THE BLUE STONE

THE BLUE STONE

an Ancestor's Tale

A. T. CONWAY

Addictive Books

Contents

PART 1

Michan Maguire   2

Chapter 1   4

Chapter 2   17

Chapter 3   28

Chapter 4   37

Chapter 5   46

Chapter 6   54

Chapter 7 - Michan   64

Chapter 8   72

Chapter 9   80

Chapter 10   88

PART 2

Chapter 1   96

Chapter 2 — 104

Chapter 3 — 115

Chapter 4 — 126

Chapter 5 — 134

Chapter 6 — 144

Chapter 7 — 150

Chapter 8 — 158

Chapter 9 — 165

Chapter 10 — 172

Chapter 11 — 180

Chapter 12 — 187

Chapter 13 — 195

Chapter 14 — 203

Chapter 15 — 213

Chapter 16 — 220

Chapter 17 — 227

Chapter 18 — 236

Chapter 19 — 246

1876 — 254

Chapter 20 — 261

PART 3

Chapter 1 - Ina Maguirre 270

Chapter 2 279

APPENDIX 288

Part 1

1847 - Ireland

Michan Maguire

When he reaches the top of the narrow track Michan stops and watches the smoke rise above the burning cottages in the distance, as the bare white land rolls down into the angry, iron sea. All of his seventeen years seem to melt in the snow around the homes of his memory. No one moves but him. No human or animal rages against the end. Even the birds have gone. All the land that he loves — his people too — rise up in grey billows and disperse across the hillside, down to the empty echoing town and across the whole of Éire. He wraps the last of his rags around him and feels only an empty ache deep inside. One day he may come back. One day the hunger must be over. He feels the smooth surface of the stone from the fairy cave in his pocket and pulls it out, holding it up to the winter sky, it's blue as intense as summer. The Tuatha can come for him if they want — there's nothing else they can take from him, so he is keeping their stone, their fairy treasure. Like the bards of old he will hold them all in his memory — all those people he had known and loved and their stories, safe, along with his mother's tales of those ancient ones. He turns then and does not look back. He has no idea what awaits him or how he will make this journey, but everyone must start somewhere. So, he begins to walk.

Chapter 1

As each step of his thin-soled boots rock and crunch through the packed snow, letting icy water in to his numb feet, memory warms him a little. His family had lived as far west as the sunset and the place had been all the world to them. Michan remembers their house in the early days. Mud bricks and straw thatch for a roof, with two rooms for them all. Six brothers in those good days — Thomas, Patrick, himself, Sean, Pol and their little sister, Ilene. He tries hard but can't bring up an image of the other brother, Cormac, drowned before he had the time to know who he was. The trapped feeling of attempts at schooling, dusty books to share, the sun streaming through streaked window-panes and the drone of an imprisoned fly or two at Father Riley's stone house by the church, surprise him with the strength of their memory. Most of the time, along with Thomas their father and their mother Ailis, they had been needed to work the farm, where it huddled snugly between the fields and the sea, not too long a walk from Sligo town. He feels again the pink burn of his skin as they worked the long days of harvest, pulling potatoes from the black earth together, the teeth-rattling shivers in the biting winds of winter, and the sharp shock of icy drops falling down at night through the thatch onto the sacking where they slept.

A thick mist rolls around him as he walks and he rubs the smooth blue stone in his stiffening fingers as it takes his memory to the bright break between harvesting and sowing.

Five brothers running off where they could, with a piece of bread each for the day, exploring hidden pathways, scaling trees, building dams and splashing through streams that snaked from cracks in the land. Sometimes they would go the other way and reach the rocky shore. One summer they had dared each other to enter the big echoing cave they found there, waves rushing and sucking within it. He smiles, remembering how their mother's stories of the Tuatha de Danaan spun around their heads that day. The powerful fairy folk who had once ruled all of Eire — wild ancestral beings — still lived for them, forever condemned to inhabit caves and the deep of rivers, lakes and seas. All the brothers, even Thomas and Patrick almost grown at the great age of ten and eleven, knew the Tuatha held feasts in their hidden palaces and they believed that if they listened hard, they could hear the fairy music. Most of all that day they hoped to catch a glimpse of the Tuatha horsemen, green mantles fringed with gold, helmets of gold on their heads and a diamond star on their foreheads. That was the day, after the fight with Patrick. Michan as loser had been dared to enter deeper into the cave and call for the riders to come forth.

He slips on the ice as he walks and remembers the slosh and suck of the water that day as he crossed the seaweed covered dune and clambered over the stony bank to get to the entrance, his brothers lining up in safety beyond, while he trembled and peered into the echoing darkness. In that moment, he had heard the music of beautiful notes plucked on strings and sung by voices without words, and he'd felt he could have stayed forever if he had wanted. A sudden deeper wave had slapped him hard then and the spell had been broken. Scrambling back on slippery feet, spitting mouthfuls of salt heavy water, he found that somehow, he was holding a piece of sea glass — a blue fairy stone —and he knew he would keep it as his secret. It was a gift from them — the Tuatha — and he would use it to call on them when he needed to.

The track becomes invisible in its snow cloak and his mind moves forward to the days just before his leaving — to the feelings he wants to chase away.

It's the last morning again. The winter sun had risen an icy yellow over the hill and for a while the snow had stopped its fall on the empty fields. Watching from behind the house he could not feel cold any longer and the hunger was a subdued beast within him. A yellow circle of his piss had spread over the ice, echoing the sunrise — and he had listened. Listening for the sound of animals lowing, snorting or stamping their feet, birds calling, and any human voices busy about their everyday world – but only silence had come back, and the cold breath of the wind.

The last of the Murphys, two cottages down, had died of the fever four days before and now only he, Ma and the last baby are left. Further down the slope of the hill he can see trails of smoke from the cottages burning. Friends from there are all gone too, goods and people, old and young, piled on a handcart, off down the wider road to Sligo and the sea. Their farmer, Mr Fell, had trudged through the snowstorm a week before, or maybe it had been longer, he had lost all sense of time by then, to tell them they must leave. The landlord had ordered his land cleared to give over to crops and animals that he could export to make money, and the cottages must go. Cleared was a strange word for burning, but with the same effect.

Michan remembers standing a minute longer breathing in the cold air, picturing again the good times they had all shared there. The green gorse springing up on the mountain in the distance one way, and the blue grey sea rolling and sparkling in the other. Long humped rows of potatoes growing in the fields and the smell of peat smoke from fires. He sees the path down to the village, primroses and gentians lining the track on the easy days of childhood play and Sunday church full of reluctant children, faces spit-scrubbed and hair watered flat by rosy faced women, up for the gossip as the last blessing finished. He did not want to leave the place. Just like the exiled fairy folk from the hillside caves he sees them around — his brothers Thomas and Patrick off to find a ship to America — no word ever sent back. Sean and Pol dead from the black fever and buried in the big grave by Father Flynn down by the church before it got too full. Then little Ilene, her five years half spent in hunger, until the hair came off her head and grew upon her face, ending so quickly as the light went out. Michan makes it stop then not wanting that memory to return of carrying the stiff child light as a bird, down to the church unable to find Father Flynn, digging a shallow grave with his own hands, covering it with earth and leaves. Frantically trying to remember the Latin words to say, sure he could see her white hand waving as he left.

He stops for a while on his journey to pick up a handful of snow and suck it melting from his red raw palms. There is a row of large stones broken at the side of the path and he sits to rest, knowing he must not get comfortable and become another nameless white bump in the bare land.

He remembers the good of Ilene then. When she had come, she had been a beautiful child. Fair not dark like the rest of them, with round blue eyes that were soon smiling at everyone, her name meaning 'light'. Anyone who saw her beauty would say, "God bless it", to ward off the evil eye and make sure that if the fairies came for her, she would be protected. She seemed to learn the stories that his mother told before she had her own language, and above all she loved music and singing. As soon as she could walk, she made up dances to the men's tunes at evening fireside feasts, and even in church she would not be still. Her hair grew in moon-silver and shining, and she would wander about in the fields and near the cottages, talking with someone no one else could see. Many people felt she must be a changeling or even that her father might be one of the Tuatha come to take a human woman to give him immortality. They would not say this near her for fear that the fairy folk came for her— or near Ailis for want of a punch.

Michan works hard to open the picture in his mind of her like that and block out the memory of the churchyard. He tries to remember the feel of the touch of her hand trustingly in his and the way she followed him whenever she could, even more when Da had gone for good and Thomas and Patrick had gone for America. She had had a way of calming beasts, even though so young, and once saved a mare of Mr Bell's by whispering to calm her so that she would not be sold away or killed. He remembers the magpie couple who waited for her to come out in the daytime and would waddle along beside her while she told them tales, and the pig she loved that lived on waste and slops and came in to sleep with the children at night. Memories of Ilene telling it stories and singing songs to lull it to sleep warm him a little, even though their power is tempered with ones of her crying for days when Thomas came home and took it to sell at market. He got money to buy bacon, ham, lard to cook with and oats, milk and grain. It was the last time they had real food. How she loved to be told the story that a beautiful fairy prince would come for her when she became a woman and she would go to dance and sing and feast in the fairy halls. If he tried very hard, he could imagine her there now and even hear the music above the January land.

Michan makes himself rise up and walk again. Tired and weak, his memory seems to weigh him down as the short day darkens.

He pictures his father Thomas, dark and wiry, but strong enough. His wanderings to find work took him away over the rolling land, sending money back and returning at times with gifts of clothes and coin for the market, and to do his duty of work for Mr Fell and for Ailis too. By the time this winter came, he had taken his chance on the government road building scheme and for a while a few pence got them milk to drink. Then he was just gone, returning no more, though there was talk he had gone as far as England to find work. His place was taken by Ilene and the last baby in the second room, and by the hunger growling in their stomachs. Ailis had become skin hung on a bony frame. She had the baby to feed and it had seemed to suck the flesh off her with the milk. The happy times of her working in the fields, making and mending clothes, gossiping with neighbour women and mashing up a pot of potatoes with milk and butter, in between comforting a child and shooing the pig and magpies away, were becoming as cloudy and as distant as the fairy caves of her stories — those places where the Tuatha, the powerful ones, were banished until they became the Sidhe, named for the caves themselves, their music nowhere to ease forgetfulness. She could no longer stride away down the stony path to the town with their best clothes to pawn until Sunday, ready for church. The only clothes they had left were torn and dirty and home for lice. This ice cold winter only the mud bricks kept the wind off them, and a boil of nettles and melted stream water kept them warm within.

Then as he walks it rises up within him – the memory of those final days.

It had begun the day after St Stephen's feast when Sean, Pol and Ilene had sickened. The boys had been out the day before looking for anything that could be eaten growing beneath the snow, or to catch a bird or rabbit with their slings, but the fever took hold that morning. Perhaps it had been within them for a while, but that was the day they both began the shivering, moaning about the pains in their legs, and crying of burning skin.

Michan feels again the rough sacking he wrapped them in and the slop of the never to be drunk water he took Ilene where she lay with her mother – very quiet – eyes open – watching him. Later he had lain on the smelly straw in the

other room and swatted lice as best he could, as much distance as possible between him and his brothers. He feels again
the pain in his chest as they had muttered of sun and wind,
tall trees and climbing on a summer hillside, until finally they
stopped at the same moment — then relief washing over him
as they had fallen into a fitful sleep. The handcart was still out
the back behind the hut and he had heaved them dead onto it
a few hours later and headed down to the church and Father
Flynn. He had taken Ilene two days later while his mother
slept. The last day.

He can't stop it from running through his mind now as
his footsteps become weaker.

Long after the feast of the Kings this day was, but by
then he had stopped counting. Ma in the bed in the second
room with the little baby. She had seemed to take Ilene's
death quite calmly when she woke in the morning, but she
would never rise from the bed again. Her shawl wrapped
around her and her hands, skeleton bony, curled and uncurled
above it.

"Come sit here and I'll tell you a story before you and
your brothers go to bed, Michan,"

"But Ma, it's morning now. We are all up and to work,"
he had lied.

"The one about the fairy rulers — you love that one you
…. and Ilene." And she had sighed.

He feels again the sacking prickling through the holes in
his trousers as he sat on the bed.

"We are ready – go on Ma!"

Ailis had begun in a voice, small but steady,

"Finnvarra was a great chief of the Sidhe, the fairy race.

He had beauty, youth, joy and power over music yet he was sad. He knew that his race had all these gifts and also power over nature, yet they were not immortal like humans. One day they would face death on earth without any hope of gaining heaven."

Her voice had trailed off then, and Michan had to ask her to go on. With an effort she had begun again,

"His Fairy Queen, called Oonagh, had golden hair that swept to the ground and she was always robed in silver gossamer, glittering with diamonds like dew drops, more beautiful than any woman on earth. But her husband was more taken with human women and charmed them to his palace under the earth — their families thinking they were dead. In the deep cave there is a palace with silver columns and crystal walls and that is where they dance and sing with the king and his knights."

Some last strength had filled Ailis' voice then, and she continued,

"I have seen her, Michan. I have heard her singing. Ilene, my only beautiful daughter — they took her and gave her the power of the Banshee — she's been sent to tell us our doom. Such sweet singing! But I must not go — I must not!"

Michan had hushed her and told her to sleep — there was no Banshee — no music or singing, and all was well. She seemed to drift off then and he had taken the dead infant she still clutched and placed it in the box it would have slept in if it had lived. Then he had left the room.

The misty cold around him fades into the distance and, in his mind, he is sitting again beside the long cold hearth, his plan beginning to form. As soon as his mother goes, or with her if she recovers, he will leave this cold and killing place that his beautiful home has become and take himself to exile like his two oldest brothers and his father. He knew that his cousin Liam Donegan had found work in England in the north and had even sent money to his family to travel over and join him. He has nothing to take but his blue stone, but he knows he can walk and which way is east by the sun in its rising and setting. He will find food in the fields and the trees, fish in the rivers, small animals in their burrows and maybe find work along the way too. Those thoughts had given him energy and he knew he must go soon, or his own strength would drain away and he too would begin to hear Ilene's song.

Later when the early dark came, he had tried to wake Ailis. She was still breathing then —her old strength that had kept them all going so long still burned somewhere. He had made a cup of cold nettle tea and drank some from the jar himself. He had tried to get her to sip a little — but he shudders as he remembers it just dribbling down into her hair. Then he had begun to sing to her a sad, beautiful song in their own language. Something finally had overwhelmed him as he sang and he had cried heaving sobs as she breathed her last. He had vowed then that, at seventeen years old, he wouldn't let himself feel anything again. He closed her eyes and stood taking the little statue of Mary and the bowl for the milk that was offered to the fairies each day. He placed them outside the door of the hut. He had dug a piece of charcoal from the remains of the fire and he carefully drew a cross on the door. Then taking one last look, he had turned away from the sea and set off along the track towards the east.

His foot sinks into a soft hole in the snow and he almost falls, tumbling back into the present. It is still daylight and he's at the edge of some water. Trees weighed down with snow lean out across the ripples and, righting himself against a trunk, he realises that he has reached a lake. He has no more strength and no fairy spells to work to free himself. He slips down the rough trunk and sinks onto the icy ground. His mind drifts, wondering whether he should walk around this lake and how far would it be, or should he just slide down into a sleep of comfort.

Jolted by a creaking, scraping noise quite near to him, he is suddenly awake. A dark shape resolves itself into a boat — his first thought — the Sidhe had not let him down after all. He struggles to his feet and slides down the icy bank towards where it bobs, entangled in some branches. It is not empty. A heavy tarpaulin decorated with ice half covers a humped shape. Under the dark canopy of trees by the lake it's hard to tell what is there, but holding onto his branch, Michan leans out as far as he can, and pulls.

The boat and its contents slide into the darkening grey of the light. The smell comes with it, the smell he knows so well —fever and death —and he follows it to the body of a man curled up in the rocking bottom. He can see the clothes are not ragged and he wears a fine pair of boots with good soles. His heart begins to pound as he knows what he will do next.

Leaning down, he finds the boots slide off easily and growing bolder he starts to pull the coat from the body's arms, but it hasn't stiffened yet and it's harder than he thinks. He climbs into the boat and grits his teeth to finish the job. Then, like a dead man from the fairy boat carried across the water for one last meeting with the living, the man suddenly rises. Thin arms wrap around Michan as they struggle in a slippery embrace which seems to last forever. As he slips from the coat, Michan pushes him hard and he goes with hardly a splash into the dark cold ripples. The boat calms its rocking with his going and the spindly body rolls around in the ice and weeds as he struggles for the safety of bank or boat. Michan thinks of reaching out to him to try and catch hold of the thrashing arms and legs, but the man floats too far out and anyway, Michan cannot swim. If he jumps into the bubbling water, they both die.

At last something seems to catch him from beneath and his stirring stops. Eyes still open, he holds Michan's gaze for a few seconds, then finally lets go and groans as he sinks down, and the water takes him.

Michan finds himself holding the coat, shaking and alone as the boat steadies. Shocked and bone-tired he fashions a bed, wrapping the tarpaulin around him and drifts off into an exhausted sleep. In his dream he has been turned into a swan like the children of the Tuatha King Lir, trapped on the lake forever by the spell of Aoife their jealous stepmother, and he has to find Ilene's magpies to release him. They are in a cave deep under the lake so he jumps in and as he sinks the arms of the dead boatman wrap around him, eyes staring straight into his, panic thrashing the water around them, until his struggling brings him up for air, the tarpaulin rolled around his face. He struggles upright, gasping, and takes stock.

It's snowing again and he sees no other banks, but only the water of the wide lake all around. Scrabbling around under the heavy cover he finds that both the oars are there and the miracle of a bag of food. Bread, biscuits and cheese poke out of the sack. Perhaps there's mould, but Michan is beyond caring and begins to stuff the gifts into his mouth stopping himself at the last minute to save some for a later meal. He looks for the poor man's body but can see no ripples or shapes floating near. For a few moments he feels the first guilt tightening his throat — but something drives him on. All guilt, all thought, must now float open-eyed somewhere in this lake — a secret that only he can hold for now. He sets off out onto the water, seeming to take an age to reach dry land, the oars slippery and blistering. The day never has a lighter point and dark comes again too soon.

Finally, the boat stops rocking and begins to bump against something. He has reached a bank. Rocking unsteadily, he shoulders the sacking bag and jumps for the solid edge — not knowing where he could be — perhaps even back to where he had started. That was when he found Kieran. A voice hissing through the dark,

"Da, is that you? You made it back — I'm here!"

Then a slight figure steps into plain view. He is almost Michan's height, wrapped in a long dark coat with a muffler round his head. The gun in his hands points straight at Michan's stomach.

Chapter 2

"Drop that bag, thief!" the figure commands, waving the gun at the sack Michan holds, then recoiling in surprise as he glimpses the boots on his wet feet. "These are his too – and his coat! Where is he?"

Michan takes in the fact that he is young—about his own age, though shorter than him and with a shaky grip on the gun. He grabs his chance and leaps on the boy; knocking the gun from his hand and kicking it into the undergrowth, he pins him to the ground. As they struggle, Michan's voice comes in gulps.

"He's dead, your Da's dead. He died in the boat—I held his hand. It was the black fever took him. He gave me the boat and the food and clothes for helping him at the end — I found a dip near the bank and laid him there — he sent me to find you!"

Lies come easy to Michan now with no one to clip him across the ear or stand outside while he is forced into confession. The lad seems to go limp underneath him then, and they both struggle to a sitting position on the icy bank.

"How do I know you're speaking the truth?" he asks in a low, defeated voice.

"Well, you don't!" Then after a pause he offers, "My name

is Michan Maguire— so now you have it you have some power over me."

They both sit in silence for a while, then a begrudging 'Kieran Quinn' comes back.

"Let's eat your Da's food, Kieran Quinn, in his memory if you like – then find that gun again. It could come in useful on our journey."

"What journey? We were heading east. Where are you going?"

Michan has no idea but chooses to seem friendly—not too much like a killer.

"East too of course – we can travel together now if you like, that's what your Da said he wanted."

He is almost believing it himself now, picturing the lad's father resting peacefully in a convenient grave, eyes closed and arms crossed reverently.

Kieran sighs, relieved that his father's last wish is being fulfilled and removes the muffler from his head revealing a thin pale face topped by straight, only slighter darker hair. He dips into the bag Michan has brought. It is easier to accept his father's death this way than anything more gruesome. Michan makes sure he finds the gun first, hidden in an icy rut behind them, before they eat the little left in the bag. Kieran's world has been moved onto shifting ground this extraordinary winter, so for now he feels he can only choose to trust this stranger. They munch on the hard cheese and solid black bread in silence. The taste of food after such a long while floods Michan's mouth, reawakening a grumbling monster in his stomach. When he feels it under control again he asks,

"Will you tell me about you and your Da then—what led you to this lake in the ice and snow?"

"We were travelling to Belfast in the east. You can get a boat there to England. It's where my Ma's family live."

"What did your Da do? Do you not have family here?"

"I did! Three sisters, dead of the measles and me away to an English run school, to escape it as well as to learn. Ma went back to England — she was too sad to stay. Da missed her and the farm was changing, workers got rid of. He'd had enough—we were going to join Ma in England."

Michan is silent for a moment as he knows how it feels to be got rid of.

"Well, you still can join her, can't you?" he asks.

Kieran begins to stand and gather the last of the food into the sack, "Her sister yes—Ma died we heard. You can die of sadness, can't you," he states.

On the weedy bank in the chill Michan silently disagrees. He has to go on. To live for all of his own lost ones.

"Da had to go back—there were important things he had forgotten. He was well when he left. He told me to wait here. The fever must have been there in him though—I should have stopped him!"

Michan feels the weight of the gun in his pocket—he has never used one but it can't be that difficult. He can dispose of this extra traveller quite easily, or he can make use of him and leave him somewhere along the way later.

"We will need money though won't we? Where's your Da's money?"

Kieran flinches. Perhaps he is to be robbed and left in a ditch after all.

"I have none. We were getting it from the bank in the town. He had enough with him until there." He steps back as he speaks. "He had an extra pocket made—wore it under his shirt."

The words hit Michan like a blow. Under that shirt, floating somewhere in the murky lake dragged down with the weight of coins entwined in the grasp of reedy fingers.

"He was too weak to tell me of it. I was only thinking of helping —I would not steal from you," he lies again. "The last he managed was that he wanted us to go on now," he lies again.

"He spoke of me though—he wanted us to go on together? He told you I was here. He must have trusted you!"

"Aye he wasn't alone." Michan paused to let the image of his selfless tending of the dying sink in. "So, do you know the road you were headed on then?"

Kieran points to the coat, "It's in there. Da kept a map in his pocket."

Michan digs his hand in and pulls a crumpled piece of paper gingerly out into the light, then flattens it on a rock. They both look it over in the gloom.

"Well it doesn't seem far by this!" he observes after a minute.

Kieran's reaction surprises him. "It's a map, stupid – an inch on this is probably five miles walking or maybe more!"

Feeling as he did when he'd been tricked by one of his brothers, Michan stands and sets his face into the wind, "Let's go then –in case those black fairy horses of the Tuatha gallop up out of the lake and trample us!" he says. But Kieran holds back.

"No—I must go over there— across the lake – give honour at his grave!" and he plants his feet, refusing to move. Controlling the feeling of anger rising within him, Michan barks,

"Would you not fulfil the final orders of your own father? He wanted us to go on!"

After a moment, Kieran nods, "Then we will go. May the spirits of the dead rest in peace," he replies to ward off both fairy horses and spirits. Michan acknowledges the reply. He knows that everyone must have heard the stories of the fierce black horses of the ancient warriors, the Tuatha de Danaan stabled below a lake, and a poor dead man buried beside the lake when he was torn apart for trying to ride them. Kieran must never know of the frantic movements and desperate glittering eyes of his own father, still floating somewhere on the cold grey ripples.

"May the spirits of the dead rest in peace," he repeats as loudly as he can, just in case the corpse can hear him.

The roads are not quiet when they reach them. Many are walking east—some with a few possessions or even a handcart carrying children, the elderly, or just the sick. The cold air cuts and often the collapsed and dying lie at the sides of the icy tracks. Sometimes, they hold out their hands to beg for help, and sometimes, the high pitched wail of a ditch- abandoned infant follows them along. They do not speak to each other but stop to take anything useful that is left on the bodies of those who have died, until by the time they reach the first workhouse by a deserted village, they have gained two shillings, a small sack of corn and a silver chain with a miraculous medal on it— the Virgin astride the earth. Kieran thinks it will do them little good, but Michan insists it will sell to someone along the way.

A crowd of desperate people clamour and beg, pushing at the workhouse gates to get in as they are shouted back by a red faced overseer waving a horse whip from the roof of a shed. Beyond them, a regular beat gets louder and a unit of soldiers appears ready to surround the increasingly frantic poor at the gate. Michan pulls at Kieran and shouts into his ear above the din,

"Round the back! There's a track there. If those soldiers catch us with money and a gun – they'll lock us up!"

Pushing their way through spiky undergrowth they come out in a place where the workhouse wall is lower and a narrow path runs through brambles. Crouching down to catch their breath they wait until the noise seems to die down. Michan indicates that they should not speak and they lean against the wall and listen. The place is thick with the hoarse shouts of the overseer, the soldiers' calls and the cries of the forlorn ghostlike people at the gates.

Michan feels for the blue glass in his pocket and smooths his fingers round it. It holds them all now – his brothers, Ilene and his mother. His touch brings them back for a while and he remembers his mother's story of the fairy grass. Whoever trod the path it grew upon would be compelled to travel on, without stopping, all through the night with restless thought and spinning ideas, over bog and mountain, through hedges and ditches until he found himself maybe twenty or thirty miles away, worn out, bruised and cut. They would have the feeling of having flown like a bird unable to pause, turn back or change its destination. In the story, the traveller ends up sad to have lost his home, but Michan still wishes he could find some of that grass.

Later, when the noise has died down, they follow the rest of the bramble path around the walls until they come to the road again. They can see soldiers guarding the workhouse gates and knots of people, some standing, some exhausted on the frozen ground, all with the heavy silence of defeat about them. They cross the road without being seen and set off again through the icy stubbled fields and long rows where hard earth would have once covered growing potato crops, following the direction Kieran's map takes them. They can move more quickly away from the crowded road but it gives less chance of pickings along the way. The first night, they find a dip in the ground under a lone hedge sheltered from the wind and eat the last of the cheese from the sack, melting snow from their hands as a drink before settling into a few hours exhausted sleep.

Next morning the sun rises, hard pale yellow in the winter blue sky and they set off down the hill towards their first town. It lies on the crossing of an even bigger lake than the one where Kieran's father floated and would normally be a busy place. Only the thin big-eyed walking corpses pass through and just one shop in the square is open. They spend one of their pennies on some corn bread and two small cellar-kept apples. There is no milk or beer.   The shopkeeper hurries them out from the gloom afterwards, telling them not to stop as the black fever is everywhere, pointing them to the road on their map. Kieran does not speak the language as well as Michan from his years at school where it was not allowed, and from his Mother's choice at home, and so they decide he should keep quiet unless English is needed.

They cross the bridge and set off east along the other bank of the lake. As the day rolls on, Michan teaches some of his father's songs to Kieran to keep them going. In some deep part of himself Michan hopes his father will step out of the long procession on the road below and join them both, black curls springing out under his favourite jaunty hat, waving and smiling as he joins in the chorus with them. He does not want to think of Kieran's father with his feeble movements and glittering eyes, leading them down to the Tuatha's cave and trapping them there forever.

That night they find a deserted looking barn and make themselves proper straw beds to rest in relative warmth. As they work at this, Michan's boot kicks something heavy and a stoppered jar rolls out into the middle of the floor. The darkness is illuminated by moonlight squeezing through holes in the roof and walls and he uses the light to work on the cork until it comes loose with a pop, spilling sticky liquid over his fingers. He tastes it tentatively, then smiles broadly.

"It's poteen Kieran – and it's all ours!" he whoops. Michan had drunk it many times at feasts and parties around the fire in the village and witnessed some fine fights as a result.

"Is it not too strong for us?"

"It will keep us warm and help us forget." They both think of Kieran's father at the same time. Settling down they make a feast of corn bread and the two bitter apples and begin to share the poteen between them.

"Tell me more about yourself Kieran," Michan probes between swigs.

"There's not much else to tell really. Da was a farmer working for a land agent. We lasted a long time until the potato crop failed and those cottiers who worked the farm began to die or leave. My school closed when the hunger grew, and illness swept through the children. So, I was sent home to him."

Michan cannot speak over the swirl of memories the words stir up.

"The landlord wanted the houses burnt to make way for livestock. He could get good money by sending them to sell in England and France—and we finally decided to leave. We were going to get a coach and travel that way in safety." Kieran hiccups. "You still awake Michan?"

"Aye!" comes back a muffled grunt.

In full flow now Kieran goes on, "So, Father decided we should join our family in England and the landlord would have to find another farmer. We only took enough food and clothes to get us to the bank and then catch the stagecoach in the town. We had the gun for safety and it was not far to the lake and quicker to cross by the boat we kept there for fishing than walk all the way round. How could I have missed that he was so ill? He could have just left the bullets. Not gone back for them as well. I would have been with him then." He sighs dramatically.

In the silence that follows, Michan's voice comes out as a whisper— "The bullets?"

"Yes – they must have been in the bottom of the boat when you found him," Kieran begins to slur.

"This gun has no bullets?" Michan voices each word very carefully. "No bullets!" For a moment they stare at each other then, both begin to laugh until tears run down their faces and gradually turn, as poteen tears often do, to sobs of sadness. When they eventually stop Michan wipes his nose on his sleeve and shakes his head slowly, "No fucking bullets!" he sighs. They share the last few sticky slugs passing the bottle between them.

"Tell me your story then, Michan." Kieran ventures when it's finished.

So he begins. Kieran passes out by the second sentence, and Michan muses it could never all be told to him anyway, so he hums a tune of Ailis' until the dark overcomes him too. Next morning they both ache everywhere and move slowly, not wanting to face daylight. Michan yelps when he stands on the discarded bottle stopper and kicks it across the floor, surprised that it rolls back instead, disappearing into the straw. Following its path, he reaches down and jumps back as his hand touches something soft.

"Look —over here—there's something!" he calls to the shaky form of Kieran just emerging from the night. Michan grabs it and pulls the material hard until soft fingers slap him in the face, the surprise knocking him off balance back onto the barn's bare floor. "Blessings of God be upon you and all your labours." He spits out the spell to ward off the evil eye, but the hand does not move again and they pull the rest of the straw away to reveal the whole of a man. He is not breathing – face still blackened by the fever that has taken him. His clothing rough and as dirty as the skin which shows.

"It was his poteen!" whispers Kieran as if they might wake him, "he must have thought himself safe here with it."

Michan, too used to handling the dead by then, sets about checking the corpse's pockets for anything worth taking. The man could well have been a thief himself as his coat turns up a shilling coin and five more pennies, although the poteen has been his only food. They cover him again and set off together with their riches on the road to the east.

As they walk, Michan considers that he might as well allow Kieran's company for now — he could still lose him when they reach the coast.

Chapter 3

The road takes them along the foot of low hills and beside the twisting shore of the lake. A pale sun shines again and the snow and ice slide into a slippery slush. They sing no songs as their feet turn to a soggy cold within their boots and nothing cools their aching heads. Their empty stomachs grumble.

Michan, who had known so much of the black fever, turns prayers around in his mind begging whoever God may be that their heads ache from the poteen and not the beginnings of illness. They trudge along amongst silent people with no energy for talk. Trees and hedges drip tears of melting ice enough for all of them. As night begins to fall they reach a small town and buy more bread and a skinny rabbit from a young boy who claims he has caught two that day and so has one to spare.

At the foot of the low hills beyond the town they find a small family in the remains of a hut, huddled around a fire, and offer to share the rabbit if they will cook it for them. The family are weak and ragged so the thought of eating meat is enough for them to agree. The man has a knife and he and Michan set to work on the skinning while Kieran talks to his wife and one small child. Aromas from the cooking churn all their stomachs, as the family have eaten nothing and drunk only melted water for two days. They tell Kieran that they were evicted from their cottage with no possessions apart from the knife and a tinder box and are heading to the east coast, down to Dublin, then on to America from the city of Liverpool in England. The rabbit spreads thinly between five of them and the bread even thinner — but they have warmth from the fire to share too. Once their feet dry out, Michan offers to tell them a story and they settle to listen, the little boy curled in his mother's shawl.

"You know that the Sidhe — the fairy race — can carry off a beautiful person, man, woman or child and when they are grown, marry them to a fairy chief or Queen," he begins.

"If the children of these marriages do not turn out well, they are sent back and others carried off in their place. Sometimes it is possible, through the spells of a powerful fairy man, to bring back a living being from fairyland. But they are never the same – with always a spirit look, having listened to the fairy music – the Ceol Sidhe – which is soft and low and plaintive and is a fatal charm to human ears. One day, a man enters a cabin and sees a young woman seated by the fire. She sings a melancholy song without settled words and music and he wonders what she means and why she never stops. He is told by her family that she had once heard the fairy harp and those who hear it lose all memory of love or hate and forget all things – forever having the sound of the Ceol Sidhe in their hearing. The man wants to know when it will stop but her family say it must never be broken or she will die. However, the man continues to question her about the music's sound and all of a sudden, she does stop and looks straight at him, 'You have broken the charm and now you must come with me back to the fairy rath'. Then she takes his hand. At once they are moving through the air with the naked fleshless feet of the spirit — both into forgetfulness of all things and perhaps the sleep of death."

Michan sighs and stretches looking around him. The embers still burn a little as everyone sleeps, and he pulls Kieran's father's coat around him and drifts off into dreams of Ilene beside a crackling hearth.

The next day, when he wakes, the family have gone and the fire is cold. The light is a little stronger every day and a watery sun outside the cabin has thawed a stream to twist and dance, newly freed from the ice. They drink from it and set off down to the road again. Groups of people still tramp along, occasionally stopping and forming a keening group around a fallen body. They move it, if they have the strength, to a ditch before travelling on again. They leave their dead no name, no cross, no record and no prayers.

Michan pulls Kieran off the path as he begins to sense that a cloud of illness covers it and he has no intention of falling ill himself. The hills are gentle drumlins around them and they mainly keep the road in view until by afternoon they reach the outer dwellings of another town.

On Kieran's map it says Clonish, but the sign just past the first dwelling holds the true name of Cluain Eos. They can see in the distance that there is what looks like an army bar-racks which will be full of red coated soldiers, so they rest on the wet trunk of a fallen tree and take stock. If the soldiers search them, they might believe the money was theirs, but the gun would land them in trouble and they could end up in prison or the workhouse. Kieran wants to keep the gun as it was his father's and he reasons it could help them if any difficult situations arose. No one would know about the lack of bullets until they actually had to shoot it. Michan argues that if they have to draw it to protect themselves then someone with a gun and bullets of their own, perhaps a soldier, would shoot to kill to protect their own life. They discuss this for a while, watching people streaming into Clonish until hunger overcomes them.

Michan had forgotten hunger for a while that winter, but now his stomach has wrapped around a little food it seems to have come back to life. The memory of Thomas and Patrick taking the cart down to the market and tossing a coin to see which brother would get to walk and which to ride, comes back to him then. He jingles the pocketed money they have found so far.

"I know! Let the coins tell us!" He shows Kieran. "When I throw it, it will either land with the Queen's head up or on its back. The head up means we keep the gun — the back showing means we bury it here and collect it when we return to our homes."

"The gun's my Da's though, Michan!" he hesitates a moment, then finally gestures agreement, "We will find it easily though when we come home – just near the sign – we can bury it!" The Queen's head decides it. They keep the gun and walk down the hill into the town.

Outside the gates of a big church near the town centre a crowd is gathering, pushing and desperate. They see the cause is a group giving out food so they join them. Some soldiers try to organise the agitated rabble until two loud shots in the air quieten them enough to roughly sort them into some sort of queue. As they near the front, they notice that people are being asked questions and some turned away. Michan feels his stomach curdle.

"Don't tell them your real name, or your age if they ask," he mutters, fearing the workhouse

"Nor which church you go to – they are turning some away!" Kieran whispers back.

Well dressed women take empty bowls back and refill them with soup to hand to the next in line. Two serious looking men question everyone as they reach the front of the line. Some are waved on and others hurried away by the soldiers. Kieran, stepping up with surprising confidence, addresses them in English, "Good day sirs. My name is James Mullen and this is my brother, John. We are on our way to our new workplace but have run low in cash. John is shy and speaks little."

Michan, keeping his eyes down, feels the beginning of admiration for Kieran's lying skills. His own accent would give him away as a traveller from the west. As the crowd grows behind them the soldiers move them on quickly — no bread is left, but they feel much improved as they walk on to the market cross. Kieran explains that the food was supplied by that particular church and they were giving it to their own people first.

"But all the people here are hungry!' Michan exclaims, waving a general hand around.

"So, they are — but how can anyone feed them all?" Kieran counters.

Reluctantly, Michan admits that Kieran is right but a feeling he can't put into words begins to grow inside him.

They use some of the dead man's money to buy bread and two eggs that are just beginning to smell, to keep them going, then head off again down the road to the east. Just outside the town a huge building glowers behind a dark wall and a group of ghost people outside its gate shows them it must be another workhouse. There are a few armed soldiers guarding it, so they choose a track around the back again to avoid them. Little cover hides them at first although no one seems to notice, until further back they find some gorse skirting which grows high enough to conceal them as they sit to eat. Michan breaks his egg carefully and drinks the contents raw, knowing they are going bad very quickly. Kieran trying to copy him, gags, until yellow yolk surrounds his face and sticks to his fingers. He finds a patch of snow under the gorse and uses its melt to clear the sticky trail into his stomach.

The map, when taken out to consult again, shows a river near the town where they can wash and drink, so, setting off they round the back wall of the workhouse and stop in shock.

In front of them stretches a deep earthen hole. Workers come hurriedly out of a gate, busy as ants on a summer path, carrying between them planks and sacks. On each plank lies a body. When they reach the hole, they are tipped off, rolling down like children on a grassy hillside, to rest at the bottom.

They look on in silent horror for a moment until Kieran breaks the spell with a cry — "Look! We passed them on the road this morning! That old man and the little child!" They watch them fall one after the other.

"Blessings of God on them." Michan uses the words to ward off the evil eye again, although it seems to have overcome any warding by then.

Skirting the pit they hurry off, not stopping until they reach a lighter place, hearts thumping. It is full of activity — more than they'd come across on their journey yet. As they get closer, they see long narrow boats waiting in a line to make headway along a busy river. Men jump on and off them and the ones nearest to a big stone built house with arched doorways are either taking sacks or boxes off their boats or collecting the same things from inside the building to fill up empty spaces.

"It's a canal," Kieran explains, "They take stuff on the boats all the way to the east and then sell it or send it to England."

"What stuff is it?"

"Well from the school lessons I can remember it's just some of everything that you can sell. Wheat, flax, animals, whatever they can load."

As they watch the men fill up the empty boats both have the same idea.

"East – they're going east!" Michan voices first.

"We could get on one – then we'd not have to walk anymore," suggests Kieran.

Neither can swim and know that if they are noticed they will be chased off or arrested— so they head for an arched stone bridge spanning the canal not far away.

It isn't guarded and they cross it purposefully as if they are on their way to work. On the other side leading up to the stores, soldiers are posted. Groups of ragged people hanging around occasionally make a dive for the doors and are roughly shoved back. They sit on a low wall and watch the sad dance as they try to work out a way in.

Michan notices a small gap where the wall doesn't quite join the building. He nods to Kieran to show him and they wait for the next rush of ragged people to distract the soldiers, then slip across to crouch behind the wall. Another rush allows them to squeeze through and they find themselves between some bushes just above the landing stage.

Workers move busily backwards and forwards loading and unloading, calling to each other, some even singing as they work. Two men nearest to them enjoy a pipe and mugs of something hot. One of them talks about going as far as Blackwater Town and the other only to Monaghan.

"Blackwater town's the furthest," Kieran whispers as they watch. The man is easy to keep in their sights as he wears a bright checked muffler and a thick, squared off black beard. His boat seems to be second in line away up the top of the platform and, after he has checked the lines and ropes tying the cover over the cargo, he goes back into the building. They take their chance, climbing onto the barge cover and crouching on the side away from the bank.

Michan finds a rope slightly looser than the others and they both work at it, hidden from the landing stage, until the gap is big enough to let them through. As Michan pushes Kieran down into the dark of the boat with the cargo he yelps, "Ow – it's biting me!"

The man is coming back leading a huge horse along the tow path. Michan jumps in too and falls onto something both soft and prickling. They struggle to tie the rope again from the inside hoping it will be convincing, as he hisses at Kieran to be quiet. At least whatever they are on is not alive. They only have to wait. A strong smell surrounds them and the crop leaves them only a few inches of air below the cargo cover. Sharp spikes stick out here and there and they have to be careful when moving. Eventually the boat lurches and rocks out into the canal. Shouts around them show there are two people working the boat – one in the distance leads the horse the other is at the back. Neither of the workers seem to have noticed the uneven rope knot and the gentle rocking begins to lull them to sleep.

Michan finds himself beside a lake in his dream. There is a boat out there but he knows he must not look at it because it contains the dead that the fairies have brought back. They wave and call to him and he tries not to look, but Ailis' voice undoes him. It is a wonderful warm feeling to see them all again and he chooses to defy the Sidhe and wade towards them. He wants so much to see them just one more time but as he does, the water becomes deeper and the warm feeling turns to fear. Becoming entangled in two arms, face to face with glittering angry eyes, he fights his way up for air. Calming his breath, he wonders how far the day has gone on, as he wakes to the feeling that the motion of the boat has stopped. He rolls over to reach across and raise a corner of the cargo cover. Outside a wall of wet bricks slides upwards as they sink down to the sound of rushing water.

He has already travelled a long way and lived through many dangers, but he realises then that this must be the end. He decides not to wake Kieran as he knows from experience that slipping into the dark in his sleep would be the easier way for him to go rather than a frantic struggle as the water takes him down. He gathers himself ready to jump, aiming to float up to the bank when the water reaches them. It doesn't.

Chapter 4

Michan feels the boat suddenly stop falling and to his relief the water comes no higher as it jerks forward with a heavy creaking sound. It rocks sideways then and someone moves across the top above them, calling out to another worker close by, which wakes a tousled Kieran with a jump. The horse snorts and jangles its harness, stamping its huge feet on the earth of the tow-path. Before Michan can work out what is happening, the cover above them is pulled roughly back and a voice speaks quite calmly,

"Come on out y' beggars—both of you!"

They squint up into the grey daylight surrounding the dark shape of the boatman. It seems to still be morning and they wince as the flax stalks they had been lying on spike their hands and ankles in their scramble to get out. The man grabs a hand each and pulls them onto the tow path just behind the swishing tail of the huge horse. Michan makes a run for it but is pulled back easily by the collar of the big coat he still wears.

"Right both of you — sit!" the man orders, "and don't try anything else!" he follows up with a kick to Michan's leg.

"We are sorry sir – we were tired – we've come a long way and still have far to go," whimpers Kieran, playing for a sympathetic reaction, but the man is smiling anyway seeming to enjoy the experience.

"Well prison would give ye a rest – that's for sure! Meg, come around here and look what we have!"

The other crew member rounds the horse and stands beside the man. Draped from head to foot in a long dark waterproof coat and wearing men's boots, she pulls off her sou'wester hat and her dark hair tumbles loose around her face. Leaning close and squinting as if she can't quite see them, she speaks in western Gaelic, "Is it insects here Da or some sort of mice got into the flax?"

They both laugh and then speaking as if Michan and Kieran weren't there he replies,

"Travellers, thieves, spies for another company, deserters from the army or murderers maybe?"

Michan's skin prickles with the thought that someone else might know about Kieran's father — someone might have seen him at the lake. Meg gives her father a playful shove.

"Stop tormenting them Da!" she laughs.

To their surprise, the bargeman then sits down beside them on the cold stones. "Tell us yer names and where yer headed lads."

"I'm John and he's James," Kieran trots out their lie, "We're going to live with our aunt in Belfast."

Meg laughs again, "If you're brothers, you must have different Da's lads – don't tell me one of you is a fairy changeling!"

Her father sighs shaking his head, "Go and make us all a brew lass – I'm fair thirsty after that last lock gate and these two deserve one last comfort before prison or the workhouse."

She strokes the horse and mutters to him gently as she walks around him to the cabin.

That remark is enough for Michan.

"We're not brothers — he's Kieran Quinn and I am Michan Maguire. I'm from near Sligo town and we met on the road. We are going to Belfast — but that's to get to England. It must be better there. There must be food and work — my Da might be there— he went away to search for both." To his embarrassment, his voice breaks up in tears at the picture his words conjure up, his mind filling with Thomas and Ailis dancing away by the fire in the cottage.

"Maguire – would that be Thomas Maguire with Ailis his wife? I knew him!" the boatman asks softly and places his hand on Michan's shaking shoulder as he nods in reply.

"My name is Loughlin – Caiden Loughlin. I knew Thomas when we were not much younger than you. We would drink together and fight! He was a tough fighter to have on your side. A beautiful singer too — could make the girls cry a treat — no wonder he got the best one for himself!"

Michan wipes his nose on his sleeve and pulls himself together. "Have you seen him in recent times?"

"No – sorry, lad. My family moved east in the first hunger – I never saw him after that."

They all accept a hot tin mug from Meg on her return and she sits down between Michan and Kieran to enjoy hers. "So, John," she directs at Kieran, "What's your story then?"

Her cheeks are a rosy pink under her smooth black hair and her eyes a deep twinkling blue. Kieran melts into the warmth of her body next to him. He tells his tale again and finishes with, "So, my father died and before he did, he sent

Michan to find me and bring me to England with him. Please don't send us to the workhouse – we've seen what happens there – the awful pit they end in all together without a prayer or even a word in memory."

Caiden Loughlin thinks a while over his brew then comes to a decision.

"If you work hard you can stay on 'til Blackwater. I can't pay you but you can share what food we've got, help with loading and unloading and locks and give Meg a hand with old Lugh Loughlin here." At his name, the huge horse snorts and swishes his tail across their heads.

Michan feels himself relax and breathe deeply for the first time in an age. He turns the fairy stone over in his pocket and thinks it might just be working against the evil eye after all. They spend the rest of the day at work, Kieran walking Lugh Loughlin with Meg, and Michan helping with the locks. He has never seen such things before and the dark swirling water and huge slippery wooden gates are more fearsome to him at first than the sea cave was when the tide had come roaring in. The heavy wooden levers fight him, with the water's power, at the filling and emptying of the lock basins. A long series of four are needed to take them downhill, Caiden explains, and they find themselves almost forgetting their journey's purpose as they work. Sometimes in the distance, they catch sight of wraithlike figures still heading along the endless road to the east, but for a while they have escaped.

At Monaghan they come to a canal warehouse and help Caiden unload a cargo of metal bolts and pieces for machinery, taking on bundles of lace bound for Belfast. The flax stems that had been their bed are unloaded too and sent to have linen and more lace made from their threads. Meg goes to fill in the paperwork and then goes off for a walk with a tall, curly haired man from the boat lined up behind them – although Caiden doesn't seem to mind.

Once she returns, they reload with wood for building, tie the covers down and head off through another set of locks. The dark comes in a little later as the days moves on, and in the dusk, they come to a high bridge which Meg calls an aqueduct. Kieran discovers a fear for the long drop beneath it and has to hide in the cabin, but Michan finds the walk along the narrow towpath exhilarating. He leans out over the tops of leafless, dark, winter trees far below, a small snake of water flowing between, and here and there a glimpse of banks still ice white in places. In his imagination it could be so easy to step off and fly— turning Lugh Loughlin into one of the Tuatha's black beauties and to gallop forever across the sky to far, magical places.

Meg walks in front to keep the beast calm and when they step back onto firm ground, Michan stays with her. No words are shared as they walk in companionable silence, in step with the great beast. A cold night sets in and they moor at a wider passing place, feed him and tie him to a ring, then fit themselves into the small cabin at the front of the barge. It contains a black stove, two blanketed bunk beds, a small table and two wooden chairs, enough for them all to sit. They warm themselves with bone broth seasoned with nettle root, wild parsley and a few carrots and onions from the pot where it has been heating for a while and a piece of black bread enough to share between four. No one speaks until the food is gone. Afterwards, Caiden gets down and digs in a box under the lower bed, producing two blankets.

"You two can sleep where we found you– there's room in there beside the lace – don't step on it!" he grunts, stretching up to open the hatch.

"Wait!" Meg stops him, "Could we not have a song or a tale before sleep Da?"

"Michan knows some good tales," Kieran pipes up.

"Of course, he would!" smiles Meg "Where he comes from, they are all bards of a sort – remembering four hundred tales each just like the ancients did."

With all eyes on him Michan can't object —so clearing his throat, he begins.

"In the time long ago, there was a king called Dagda. He was the father of all the Tuatha de Danaan and had many wonderful powers and weapons and in particular, a beautiful harp made from rare wood, gold and jewels. The harp would play only for Dagda and its music held people spellbound. Like all the Tuatha, Dagda had to go into battle against the Formorians who were trying to take our beautiful country from them. Now, there came one particularly difficult battle and all the Tuatha warriors had to fight, leaving their great hall unattended. The Formorians broke in and seeing the beautiful harp there, they took it, hoping it would help them control their enemies. But it only worked for Dagda of course. The Tuatha were able to chase the Formorians down and recover the harp. Dagda burst into the hall where they were feasting, believing they had won the battle, and called to his harp to jump into his arms. He then played the magical chords — the Music of Tears made the whole hall wail in sorrow; the Music of Mirth made them laugh hysterically; and finally, the Music of Sleep made them all fall into a deep and lasting slumber. Although the Formorians were not defeated forever, they slept for some time and the Tuatha could roam freely across the land."

As he finishes, Kieran and Meg are half asleep themselves, and Caiden says quietly, "My thanks to the beautiful Ailis for that, son."

They open the hatch then clamber over the boat, the cold air rushing in as sharp as a Formorian sword. Michan lies awake by the lace for quite a while, listening to the night noises and the music of tears.

When he wakes near dawn from a dream of magpies picking at glowing white lace that turns into bones, he has the feeling whispering voices have saved him from something; but Kieran is still sleeping and the boat calm and steady. Lifting a corner of the cover he peeps out and sees there are two people on the bench beside the path. They murmur and laugh then begin to move in a slow seated dance. As he watches, a cloud scuds away from the moon and for a moment he sees the faces of Meg and the man from the canal warehouse. He cannot understand why it makes him feel sad, for they seem happy indeed, but he pulls the corner of the tarpaulin back down and lies back wrapped in his blanket, for some reason thinking of the pig and the safe place by the fire when his father had been at home.

Next day, they journey on to towards Blackwater where the lace will be taken off and Caiden tells them that he will arrange with one of the carters there to take them on into Belfast town. Michan is becoming a good hand with lock gates and when not crossing an aqueduct, Kieran is learning a new skill controlling Lugh Loughlin, who is not always willing to perform as he is told. They reach the docks at Blackwater in the late afternoon and Caiden agrees to let them have one more night on the barge while they are docked. The company do not allow passengers and someone at Blackwater would be sure to report them if they wanted to stay on and travel further.

The night is a little warmer than it has been and wrapped in blankets and their great coats they sit out on the tow path building a fire to cook a sausage each that Meg has managed to get from the town. The beer is good and Meg's friend Seamus, who has joined them, brings poteen as well, so after a while they all begin to sing the old songs. Caiden surprises Michan and Kieran by pulling out a tin whistle and plays a jig or two. A mixture of tiredness and poteen leads the songs down a sadder and sadder path until Michan sings *The last Rose of Summer*. Then they all join in *Fainne Geal an Lae*, which Kieran recognises as *The Dawning of the Day* and sings the last verse loudly in English ending with,

"And the morning light was shining bright

At the dawning of the day."

A warm silence wraps them all for a while after this, until Caiden rises and fetching a pan of water, pours it over the hissing remains of the fire. He hums the last lines of Kieran's song over again as he pulls up the hatch, then halfway in, he stops and calls, "I hope you find your dreams lads! Warm hearth, hot meals, soft beds, work for your hands and a good woman each eh? Now get inside for the cold has come, whether you can feel it or not!"

Then he closes the hatch over his head leaving Meg to wander off somewhere with her man and Lugh Loughlin to snuffle and shift in his sleep. The boat rocks Michan and Kieran gently for the last time, and the night seems to flash past until they hear Meg return and then they are standing in the dawn beside another horse, attached to a cart this time, meeting Joe Byrne, the carter, who is to be their ride into Belfast town.

They clamber sleepily up onto the back of his cart and keep their eyes on Meg and Caiden's waving figures framed against the shape of Lugh, until the cart turns out of the canal yard and they are lost from sight.

Chapter 5

The first night they sleep in the soft nest they make amongst the bundles of lace. Next day, the clachans seem to join together and grow into a busy town. Cold air swirls around and the horse jangles and snorts as Michan takes it all in. A black mountain stands guard over the rest of the rows of buildings sleeping at its feet. They are soon surrounded by small streets of houses – some made of clay and lime and others tall and of imposing brick with glass windows draped to hide the lives of the inhabitants from the pain of the streets. Joe Byrne curses at times as he negotiates piles of foul-smelling waste and shouts at ragged people wandering or hurrying around them through the bustling streets. To Michan it looks little different to Sligo, Clones and even the little villages along their way. He hopes to get work here in Belfast – enough to feed himself and pay the passage to England, but the groups of pale and hopeless wanderers show that might be difficult.

Joe pulls up alongside a bigger, pink painted building and stretches himself before jumping down.

"C'mon lads! Let's get this stuff into the store house here and then your job is done."

As usual, Michan has to wake Kieran, who seems to be

able to sleep deeply anywhere – and they set to work. In less than an hour Mr Burn has given them the shilling each he'd promised for their help and points them to a set of yards and courts where he says they will find lodgings and food, as well as directions to the first steamer going out.

They watch the cart move off into the busy street and turn to face the yard behind them. Lennan's court is a sort of square. Piles of dirt of every sort form hills on the slippery cobbles, while above them lines of grey washing flap and waft the smell around. The houses must once have been white-washed but are now patterned with cracks and smoke stained from factory chimneys. Joe Byrne had told them to go to number twenty three which is owned by a Mrs Brennan, and to say that he sent them for a bed. Unsure which one to approach as there are no numbers visible, a door flings open and a pinch-faced woman with a black shawl over her head calls, "You two wanting a bed then? England or America is it?"

Crossing the stones with care, they approach her.

"Are you Mrs Brennan? England it is —we'll not want more than two or three nights—Mr. Joe Byrne sent us here."

She looks them up and down while other hidden eyes send prickles down their necks, then she sniffs,

"Aye that I am! You have money I take it? Joe wouldn't've sent you otherwise – and I can see you have two good coats and boots about you. Upstairs – room on left – sharing with four more. There's not much food but there is a stirabout at six o'clock and a piece of black bread for breakfast. Water in the well over in the next yard. A shilling each for six days, then two more when you get work or a steamer ticket— or you're out."

She finishes, then holds out her hand and waits. After handing the coins over, they follow her inside and up a dark staircase. Two doors flank it at the top and she points them into the left one then hurries off. Inside the room they can almost touch each wall from the doorway. Damp grey wallpaper hangs down in places and condensation makes snail tracks down the greasy windowpanes which let in a little of the cold light. Squashed together on the wooden floorboards are six boxes lined with straw and covered with a piece of sacking.

There are no occupants or possessions to make a claim on the spaces, so they make their way back down to the bottom of the stairs and into a room the same size as the one up above, where a cold hearth flanks a table which holds a heavy iron tea pot. In the corner, two small children sit on a crate, silently eyeing them – their clothes ragged and hair thinning in a way that makes Michan's heart contract. "Hello cairde beaga. Where has your mother gone?" he asks them gently. They only stare back, wide eyed, until Kieran says,

"Perhaps they don't speak the language – or are deaf? We are in the east now you know." He tries the question in English but the response is just the same. There seems little else they can do so they decide to leave and see some of the city, hoping Mrs Brennan will be back when they return.

Outside the Court they soon come to a wide street. Carriages and laden carts pass them and people of all sorts walk by or huddle against the walls. Some are dressed in a way Michan has rarely seen with tall hard hats and tailcoats below fine bushes of whiskers shaped and shined with oil. Few women are about but they see shawl covered versions of Mrs Brennan passing by, busy with baskets amid the groups of people by the walls, their clothing hanging ragged and torn above stick thin legs and bare blackened feet. Michan shivers, "It's here too – the hunger – look around Kieran. We cannot rest here for long or it will catch us and snuff us out."

"Maybe we need to call on a Fairy King or ancient hero to carry us away from here?" Kieran sighs, then takes to marvelling as they turn a corner and find themselves in an even wider road. Tall buildings line a crossroad and they have to stop and look up to take in their solid regular brick work and rows of glinting windows. Coloured awnings hang down over the base of some of them protecting goods for sale and long glass windows hold more goods, described in writing, which Kieran reads aloud. Michan stands in front of one trying to make out what a 'Milliner of Superior Standard' makes, until the shapes in the dark within form themselves into hats and gloves – a whole shop just for them. Tall hard hats, rounder shiny ones and a glittering straw one with ribbons and feathers lie in a row along a green draped shelf and when he stands back a little, Michan can see the shape of himself clearly. A thin white face, dark sunken eyes, the few hairs of an early beard and a bush of dark curls sticking out above a long shabby coat reaching to dusty boots. His father Thomas— just as he'd last seen him – that's who he is now! The shop door opening catches him in the mirrors of angled glass and the image of Michan-Thomas casts itself a thousand times into the future and the past. His brain takes a few moments to understand what he sees and he nods to them all for it seems right. Then the shop door shuts and they are gone.

Further on, a man on a corner plays a fiddle and a small child dances a jig to it, pretty and desperate. It feels rich giving them a penny for their troubles and both hope they will not regret it later. Amongst the passing people are groups of travellers, thin, pale and ragged; they speak to each other in the Irish that Michan knows well. All seem to be heading in one direction and more than once he hears the word for 'ship' pass amongst them. A group of them in front of a bakery have stopped in concern as one is lying on the ground. An old man, his last few white hairs trailing from a bare head and his gnarled feet bare, looks to have given up. The group gathered around him coax and pull, trying to raise him up until three men appear in black coats and caps and push them away. "Back against the wall!" one of them commands the group, while the other two check the old man.

"Looks like exhaustion Sergeant – not the fever."

"They're for the workhouse then – not the hospital," the sergeant replies. He stands and with slow careful words addresses the group, "Do any of you have money?"

Three women with a young lad and little girl just stare at him until Michan makes a move towards them but is stopped by Kieran holding him back, "No, don't help them! It'll be us for the workhouse next. Then we'll catch the fever and end up in a pit – remember?"

One of the policemen knows the word for money – airgead— and repeats it louder and louder. By then a crowd has gathered and the old man stops moving. They have no money of course and are moved off in a slow procession with two policemen carrying the old man by the arms and legs while the women begin to keen. As they pass, his glittering eyes seem to pierce Michan and he shivers.

They hurry off in silence for a while, then pass the rest

of the day avoiding any policemen, weaving their way through the unfamiliar streets and resting for a while beside a river until, as evening draws in, they find the ramshackle houses at the entrance to Lennan's Court again. Children's voices and a man's shouts come from somewhere and factory chimneys point smoking fingers into the lowering sky.

Reluctant to go in, Michan leans against a wall.

"Tomorrow let's find a boat. If we wait here looking for work it will be us next for the workhouse or an end like the poteen man in that barn."

"Tomorrow we should for sure – we have that money of his still. We can ask Mrs Brennan the cost of a ticket. We need to get to England now!" Kieran coughs. For the first time since they left the Loughlins at the narrow boat Michan let himself hear it.

Inside number twenty three Mrs Brennan has returned and the small room is full of hot smoke and sweat from three workmen squashed around the table. A fire crackles in the grate throwing dancing shapes across the two children still sitting on the crate as if they had never moved. Mrs Brennan stirs a pot of something which resembles slime with greyish lumps drowning and resurfacing around the spoon. She ladles it into wooden bowls for each of them and indicates that they should push onto the benches each side. No attempt is made to introduce anyone and no one speaks. The last drops fill a cup each for the listless children who share a spoon to dig for every lump. Michan and Kieran are well used now to swallowing down anything which might cut their hunger, but even they have to try not to grimace as the stirabout goes down.

"You two take the plates to the pump in the next

yard," Mrs Brennan directs them, "and be thankful for God's bounty—we had some milk today to add to the starch sowens — so you'll be satisfied 'til morning!"

When they get back the three men are already settling under their sacking in the boxes nearest the bedroom door and they have to climb over them to reach the empty ones.

Michan lays awake in the hard box, the starch churning his stomach, his ears full of the men's snores and Kieran's coughing. He closes his eyes and uses his story mind to turn the snoring to the sound of waves and the coughing to rattling stones on the shore. Time slides away and he is back on the beach in front of the cave mouth, a pale figure beckoning him from within. He wants her to be Oonagh, the queen of fairies, but she turns into Meg Loughlin. She wears a glittering diamond dress, a wreath of greenery in her hair and holds the reigns of a beautiful fierce black horse who seems to be Lugh Loughlin in a new shape. As he nears her she smiles and he can see all her body beneath the diamond layer. He knows he can kiss her if he wants but she steps aside and behind her there is a long table laid out with golden plates and bowls of fruit of many shapes and sizes. Ham, bacon, chicken legs, small white fish and soft white bread lie there, amongst other foods he does not recognise. Oonagh-Meg whispers in his ear, 'eat and you can kiss me, then stay here in my rath — dance, eat, take pleasure to your fill and you need never ever go back'. At this, fear seems to grip him and he tries to break away. He steps back and begins to fall into the churning waves below. As he sinks and struggles and fights for breath, she watches him, smiling. His own groan wakes him, thrusting him back onto the prickling straw and a harsh voice from the dark snaps, 'Leave it alone, y' little beggar. 'Tis blind you'll go!'

Next morning all the men have gone when they wake, so in the kitchen they eat another bowl of stirabout – even harder to swallow cold – and gathering their few possessions, they leave. Mrs Brennan tells them the best way to the docks where they might find work or a place on a steamer. They refuse her offer of leaving their sack with her as they both suspect it will not be there when they return, and if they can get on a passage to England they have no intention of doing that. The children are not about and to show some courtesy Kieran asks after them.

"Long gone to work – they must earn their keep." She almost smiles.

"Aye indeed, Mrs." Michan nudges Kieran not to speak again. "May God's blessings be with you. Come on Mr Quinn – to work with us too!" and they walk out into the grey light – not knowing that Lennan's Court will soon seem as luxury to them.

Chapter 6

It's still early but out in the broad central street, life is already bustling. Smaller groups flow together into a crowd as they near the port. Hand carts are piled high with belongings, the very young and old dotted amongst them. Their purpose is to leave, barefoot or well-shod – to escape the hunger, even if it means scattering from beloved places forever.

'How many of these can a steamer take?' Kieran wonders as his spirits fall. 'Sure, this crowd would sink a pretty big boat, I suppose – and this won't help'. He nods towards black coated police who are beginning to surround them.

Two men near them overhear their conversation and tell them that they know a way round to the front if they want to follow. They speak in Michan's Irish, so he is for trusting them. They follow slipping and twisting through the back of the crowd until they reach a dark stone archway. Once in the slippery alleyway, the men suddenly stop and turn, causing Kieran to stumble into one of them who grabs his arm and twists it behind his back in a swift movement that doesn't hide the glint of the knife thrust at his throat. Michan freezes.

"Right lads – you can die here now, and no one will ever know who you were – or you can take your chance with charity. What's yer choice?" the knifeman hisses. The second man's knife grazes Michan at his back,

"Do not move or speak!" His whisper is almost intimate, and his free hand runs all over Michan's body, digging out the last two pounds and three pennies and slipping the strap of his sack off his shoulder.

"There's a gun in here, Kevin – a fecking gun," he breaths, "Some nice coin too. It's England for us today!" He tosses the bag to Kevin, who lets Kieran go. "We're not murderers, lads." The other man laughs, "Go now and keep going, or we might try it for a bit of sport."

They run back into the grey daylight and the open square. Leaning against the nearest wall, Michan fights the stirabout from rising into his throat while Kieran folds up in a fit of coughing, one hand covering up the blood from the nick in his neck. People shuffle away from them, and in the space they clear, two police officers stand.

"Stay where you are!" commands the tallest one as Michan attempts to bolt.

"So, what is this here?" demands the other officer through a thick ginger moustache, tapping his baton slowly against his other hand.

"We were attacked – down there – they have knives!" gasps Kieran, showing the blood on his hand.

"Did they steal anything valuable?" asks ginger moustache. Michan elbows Kieran before he can reply.

"Only our money officer. We had it saved from our family to pay for the boat to England. They took it all."

"So, you have no means to live now?" asks the taller officer. "Come on, answer – there's much to be done today lads – we can't loiter here!"

"But are you not going to chase the robbers? One was called Kevin – we can describe them for you," Kieran insists.

Ginger moustache waves at the crowd behind them, "There's not enough of us today, and we've got a crowd to sort through here. If they've got your money, they'll be gone soon enough. Then they're England's problem. Now, over there with both of you."

They are ushered roughly towards a horse and cart waiting in the street and told to get in. A thin-faced man in another uniform takes their names— John and James Connor this time— and tells them to remain where they are until the rest are sorted. A very young policeman with a gun stands at the back of the cart and watches them coldly. They speak quietly in Irish to each other.

"We're lost now – this is for the workhouse." whispers Michan, "We couldn't have let them chase those bastards, or they'd have found the gun and worked out we had a lot more money than the fare to England."

"How will we ever pay for the boat now, Michan? Even if we can escape," sighs Kieran, "Sometimes I wish for my father back so much. He would know what to do."

"Blessings on his spirit," Michan automatically crosses himself. "Let's hope he doesn't come back. We do not need a shade to set our teeth chattering as well, do we?"

After the thin-faced man has filled the cart with people, he and the young officer jump up front, then they set off past the shops and awnings and the gazing windows. No one speaks, and people in the street cross hurriedly out of their way. They pass where they had walked in hope the day before, even glimpsing the entrance to Lennan's Court as the cart begins to go uphill. A set of high metal gates loom in front of them. No crowds wail and struggle as they had at the other workhouses they had passed on their journey. Beyond them, a long avenue curves through a neat green lawn to a grand ornate building. Halfway to the house they give way to two more carts going in the opposite direction— their subdued passengers holding brushes, pails and shovels. Rounding one of the building's broad wings, they pull up in a yard filled with activity.

Wooden huts stretch away behind the place, many still being constructed. The overseer tells them all to get down and wait in line, disappearing into the main building. Some of the workers call a greeting to them, and as they pass by carrying a long plank, two of them stop and speak. Michan hails them, "Dia Duit! Are you inmates, or are you builders here?"

The lead one, small, thin and pale as snow answers,

"Sure, we work, and they give us a meal, then we go and try for the night shelter. If we get in, it's a shared bed and a little more food, then it is back here to queue for work the next morning – but this is better than some of the jobs, cara!"

"How so?" chips in Kieran, but the overseer has come back and gives them all numbers for the groups they should be in — snapping at the workers to get back to their jobs.

They are relieved to be together in group seven with two hard-faced women, six men of varying ages, and one older man in rags, who seems to be almost fainting. Someone hands them their brushes, shovels, and buckets and tells them they are going back out on the street for the rest of the day to earn their evening meal. Two officers go with them, O'Neil, the young one, and an older, fatter man called Watson. They rattle through streets — some beginning to become famil-iar— and stop at a place very like Lennan's Court. Watson and O'Neil chivvy them off and tell them what their jobs will be.

"Clear the midden heap from this yard then another five along the row – all of the shit mind. Then whitewash the houses that run along the main street. We like things to look clean and pleasing here. It is the charity of this town that's keeping you alive now. Anyone who wants to leave, think twice. It could get you to the charity of the House of Correc-tion instead."

As Watson gives the orders, O'Neil taps the handle of his gun and looks directly at Michan and Kieran. So, they work. One of the women holds the barrow while Michan and another man shovel the foul-smelling heap into it. When it is full, another woman takes it and empties it into their cart, then it all starts again. Kieran brushes flagstones then swills them down with buckets of finger numbing water from a pump. The police officers occasionally shout at anyone they consider slacking, particularly the elderly man.

"Come on, Seamus! Work for that supper!"

By the end of the day, as they hear the local clocks chime five, every bit of their bodies ache. The cart trundles off with its load of manure, and they have to walk back, shoul-dering tools or pushing barrows as they go. Handing them back, they are given a ticket and sent to another line for food. They have made it through the first day — the bowl of stew at a crowded table their reward. The old man lies with his head down beside his bowl, and several people already have their eye on finishing it. A young lad shakes him awake and tries to spoon it into his mouth, begging, "C'mon Da! Tis a fairy feast for you!"

Michan eats quickly, blocking out the choking gasps, ready to spring on the bowl if the man collapses, but he rallies enough to finish his bowl. They are all moved on after that to make way for the next sitting and they are herded to a steam-filled bathhouse. Their clothes are now their only possessions, and they want to keep them, but have no choice but to strip naked and queue with the other men.

"We have to deal with the lice lads," another attendant tells them – this one round and rosy, "Just get it over with. Leave all your clothes on this side. They will be burned – you'll get more when you come out."

"I need my coat," Michan almost whimpers.

"We can put it to wash. If it doesn't fall apart, you can have it back," comes the almost kindly reply, so they move on. Michan slips the blue fairy stone from the pocket of Kieran's father's coat before he drops it – the robbers did not get it, and the workhouse isn't going to either. The steaming water is hot and white with a strong soap to kill the lice, but it eases all their aching for a few minutes, and it is entertaining to watch the lice jump off and drown in torment.

On the other side, there is a rough wet towel, some ill-fitting clothes and a blanket, then directions to find a bunk in one of the huts. As Michan struggles to find a pair of boots from a pile, he is tapped on the shoulder by a tall young man, as thin as all the others, wet brown hair dripping into green eyes, and soaking his rough cloth shirt. He holds a calloused hand out, and even in the steamy air, Michan can see the beauty of his blue fairy stone resting there.

"This is yours—I saw you drop it. Here, take it! It must be worth something to you. If it were mine, I would not want to lose it." He takes it with gratitude in that mixed feeling of relief and disbelief when finding something precious which you did not know was lost. They walk together to the huts with Kieran and discover his name is Felim. He is a married man, but his wife and children are in the other side of the workhouse. Like every inmate, he says he is only there for a short visit and will soon move on. His brother and father are in prison waiting to be sent away as convicts, and he wants to get to see them one last time.

"What is it they have done?" Kieran asks.

"Let hunger drive them, I suppose. They stole a loaf and a jug of milk, but the farmer caught them in his pantry. My little sister was the lookout, but she fell asleep."

"Is she in prison too?"

"No lads—she died of the cold, hiding from the soldiers. I never saw her again. I have the story from someone who knew us—'tis too sad to talk of. Here's a hut that's got some spaces. Let's get in."

The place soon fills up with aching bodies curling under rough blankets in the hope their wet hair would soon dry as they bid goodnight to Felim. Somewhere a man hums a gentle air of home, and it rises above the coughing and restless creaking of the bunks. The wind gathers strength from behind the Black Mountain, scattering cold sleet on the roof.

Five days pass in the same way. Michan begins to grow healthier with regular food and long nights of rest, though

Kieran's cough becomes more frequent. Each evening they share stories with Felim and the others in their hut who have not already fallen into the sleep of exhaustion. He tells them of the beginning, with Indian corn causing rotten stomachs, relief work from the English government ending, evictions from their homes, and once the potatoes failed, no food at all. Michan and others tell of mass graves and burial without funerals as they all share the desire to get away somehow. Another man even has tales of people eating rats and dogs and the bark from trees to try and cling on to life. Winter has come back bitterer than before, and their feet and fingers ache with it. All have lost people dear to them, and talking of their lives in the dark night time of the hut helps a little.

On the sixth day, they are lined up and given a number again – a one or a two this time. Michan and Felim are a two and Kieran a one, but they manage to confuse the overseer into slipping him into group two as well, and wait to find out what the numbers mean.

He explains crisply, "We have too many destitute and sick needing help now, so we have decided that those of you in the second group are classed as able to work. We have a day and night shelter you can apply to, or you can make your way back to the places you came from. You will be able to take a coat from the recovered pile and some bread and cheese for today. The first group remains here."

Relief and apprehension flood over them. "Well, at least we get out of here alive – not planted in that big hole they're digging over there!" enthuses Michan.

"Luck go with you boys—I'm away to find my Siobhan, then off to visit the prison together with the children and then on to find a place on a boat. Perhaps we'll meet you in England one day?" Felim waves to them and hurries off to the other side of the building.

"Aye, perhaps," Michan calls after him, but knows he will come back to Eire once he finds his father and somehow puts the remains of his family back together. Kieran's father's coat is gone from the pile in the shed, so they make do with what they can find and walk with springing step along the curve of the driveway, dodging new cargoes of the silent and the soon to be dead. They do not see Felim fall to the ground at the news of his wife's death or hear his shouts as they keep him from his children in the sickbay.

Wandering down to Lennan's Yard, they catch its midden smell more pungently than before. The work parties have not reached it yet, and they are hoping Mrs. Brennan will give them the rest of the board that she owes them. A rare sun shines from above the sagging slate rooves and shows the walls' smoky dirt, colouring in the mud cracks on the stone tiles. No one answers at number twenty-three. The door swings loosely at their touch, so they go inside. The kitchen is cold and empty, and upstairs the boxes smell of old straw and rat droppings. Memory begins to grip Michan. "This brings to mind my home – the way it was when I left!"

"They could all be out working," whispers Kieran

"Maybe," Michan leads them back down the narrow wooden stair, "but Mrs. Brennan would surely be around somewhere— we can wait for her."

Outside they crouch on the tiles, eat the small meal of bread and cheese the workhouse sent them off with, and wait. After a while, Michan stands up and goes to the midden to piss. After he finishes, he walks around to avoid the wettest bit, then suddenly stops and lets out a low moan; "Oh look cara, look!" His voice shakes as Kieran jumps up to join him.

Sticking out of the midden is the top of a head and a small white hand. They do not stop to ward off the evil eye, but run without thought until entirely lost.

Chapter 7 - Michan

As they pant to a halt, the black mountain looms closer and red brick houses surround them — each standing at the top of a gleaming flight of stairs. A wide road runs between these, the occasional carriage passing to and fro. A ringleted little girl waves and smiles from one of them, and a man in a tall hat and tail-coat nods to her as he passes. The row ends with a wooden gate which opens on to a mud track. Two pigs snuffle contentedly in the field behind it and a few chickens squawk and squabble in a fenced off run. Michan and Kieran climb the fence and sit down on a bench under a bare tree, out of sight of the houses. They let their hearts settle in their chests. Kieran struggles to keep his cough under control as they take in their surroundings. Neither can speak the thoughts in their minds. There are no words for those strange silent children.

After a while, Michan begins to tell one of Ailis' stories. It has been waiting in his mind since the canal.

"Long ago, there was a beautiful land in the western sea. People called it Tir na Nóg; the Land of the Young. The trees there were always green, the flowers were always in bloom, and the men and women never grew old. This is the story of Oisin, who was the son of Fionn MacCumhail, himself a great fighter and a leader of the Fianna. One day, Oisin got to travel to Tir na Nóg. It was a day when the Fianna were hunting deer on the shores of a lough and had taken a rest on a hilltop when a beautiful girl came riding towards them on a snow-white horse. Her clothes were rich like a princess, and her long golden hair hung down to her waist. As she drew near, Fionn called out to her, "What is your name, and what land do you come from, lady?"

"I am Niamh of the Golden Hair, and my father is the king of Tir na Nog," she replied, "I have heard much of a warrior called Oisin, and I have come to find him and take him back to the Land of the Young with me."

Fionn did not want to let his son go, but Oisin had already fallen in love with Niamh, and he jumped on her fairy horse and left with her. They travelled a long way over rivers, lakes, hills and mountains, moving swiftly as a shadow until they reached her land. There they lived in perfect happiness for three hundred years until a great longing came on Oisin to go back to Eire, to his native land. Niamh warned him that to set foot even once on the soil of Eire would mean he could never return to the Land of the Young. Oisin had the idea that he would ride a fairy horse and never dismount, thus not setting foot on the ground, and so he set off on his journey. When he got there, all his family had gone, and there was no trace of Fionn or the Fianna. Everything had changed. Not knowing what to do, he rode on a little further and came across some men needing help to move a heavy rock. Now, Oisin was powerful, but as he tried to help the saddle strap on his horse broke, and he tumbled to the ground. Instantly he became old and withered and could only babble of the Fianna and Tir na Nog to people who knew nothing of them—until soon he died."

In the silence that follows the story even the pigs lie down to rest, and Kieran sighs, "Tis us that are like Oisin — we can't go back for everyone has gone — we must go on. Perhaps England is our Tir na Nog?"

"Perhaps – we have surely travelled far, cara." Michan stretches and yawns, then a voice behind them speaks.

"La maith. Good day. No, stay seated — don't run!" A young woman moves into view — dark hair tied up in a bonnet, and clothes of fine make about her.

"My name is Jane. I am visiting the house up there behind us. I love your story, but my Irish is not up to understanding all of it – could you tell it again in English? I won't send you away or let anyone know your hiding place – I promise."

As there seems to be little to lose either way, they decide to trust her and run if they need to later. Michan begins again while she perches on the end of the bench and listens intently. He finishes in Irish to Kieran, "Be ready to run if we have to. She'll be easy to push over."

"I promise you there is no need to run – you are safe here. I got 'push' and 'run' quite well there!" she laughs. "Thank you for the tale. Now wait here, and I will find you food and a place for the while. I imagine from your clothing that you have come from the workhouse and don't want to go back there. You would have problems finding the night shelter from here." They nod and watch her retreat.

"Go or stay?" Kieran asks.

"We'll give her a chance –it seems like she might be a

do-gooder like the people with the soup, but she loved Oisin's story, didn't she?"

The pigs have woken and snort in the mud, while the hens and their cockerel enjoy a noisy argument. A wind picks up around the black mountain and shakes the skeleton arms of the tree.

Jane returns with a basket and blankets.

"Come with me. There is a place you can stay in exchange for clearing up the alley and outbuildings. It's my cousin's house, but her husband is away at the moment, so it's safe for now."

She leads them to a small mud-brick building nestled in a dip in the field. Inside is colder than outside. Straw on the mud floor glints in the light from the door, and a brooding black grate awaits a fire. Jane explains that a family had lived in it, but her cousin's husband had sent them away for fear of fever when the hunger came. Her cousin said they were off to America she thought, but no one heard from them again. Michan crouches down by the grate, his thoughts churning. However far he travels, he comes back to this – a cold hut, fears of fever, and straw for a bed. Turning the blue fairy stone in his fingers, he thinks of home.

"It is not much, but you will be safe and fed for now." Jane seems to pick up on Michan's thoughts, but Kieran says firmly,

"We will stay until we can find a way to get to England, Miss – you are kind." She leaves them to eat, and they do so in silence except for Michan's muttered, "Poteen instead of this milk she gives us—now that would have been kind!"

Days of cleaning, hammering, sawing and painting, and

evenings of storytelling roll on as the ice comes back, freezing their legs and cracking their boots. While not openly stopping them from leaving, it is clear that Jane does not want them to wander out into the streets, and they wonder if she is protecting them from the world or a danger worse than famine and fever. They grow to like her over time, with her ink-stained fingers and her interest in all they have to tell. She speaks as someone educated in England or at an English school and tells them she comes from Dublin and will go back there in the summer. Her cousin has been ill with her nerves — something Kieran understands from his mother's sadness — and she has come to help with the little daughter while her husband is away. She encourages them to tell her their own stories, not just the ancient people's tales, and she scribbles them down by candlelight.

"You are writing a story," Kieran comments one evening after Michan sings a sad song of longing and loss to them.

"I am writing your story," she smiles, "and the story of our country."

"A whole book?"

She seems lost in thought for a moment, "One day a book. But this is for a newspaper. It's time the owners, the agents, the rulers know the truth about this place. About what is happening to the country." Her voice rises with each word until she almost shouts the final ones. "Don't forget boys – don't forget when you get to England – tell everyone. Your voices must be raised!"

For a few moments afterwards, the silence hovers wrapped in gentle crackling from the grate – then she collects her pen and inkpot and stands up. "Good night," she mutters quietly, her back to them as she leaves.

Kieran sighs, "She's like a man. She talks like one – like a rebel!"

"She is a woman, though, born to money. She's set for marriage, bearing children, for owning nothing but what is his. For being ruled, not ruling. She'll soon forget us— or lose her voice in our favour."

Michan's words come out of the last glow of light from the dying embers. "We must go soon."

The last Sunday in the cabin, as the bells ring out for service and Mass, loud voices shouting and doors banging alert them to danger. There is no time to run or hide before the door flies open and a well-dressed man strides in, calling over his shoulder,

"They are here! The vermin! They carry it with them! How long, Jane? How long have they been living here on my property — eating my food?" He grabs at whatever part of them he can and drags them out, throwing them down in the mud at Jane's feet.

"Do not move! Do not attempt to get up! Oh god, Jane, do they even speak English?" Michan answers in Irish, "Not for him – the bastard!"

"He is asking you to let them up," Jane mistranslates," They are cold and wet." Her usual strength seems to have left her, and she is pleading with this man.

"Very well, but tell them no running – my servant has a gun, and doubtless, no one will know they are gone with a bullet and not the usual fever."

"This bastard is my cousin's husband – he means what he says," she says in Irish.

"Get up and face me!" the man demands, flecks of angry spit appearing as he does. Jane nods to them to obey.

"My child has measles – you layabouts and beggars bring it with you. She may die because of you." He turns to a servant, "James – lock them up in the empty stable, then arrange for this shed to be pulled down. Miss Elgee, I will deal with you later – go back inside."

James shoves them roughly into separate stalls, bolts the big doors shut, and leaves. Outside, the churches still ring out to the faithful their message of love, repentance and salvation, and sleet begins to patter on the roof. They have run out of hopeful thoughts and escape plans and sink onto the flags beneath the empty manger to wait for the police.

A while later, the big stable door creaks open, and a dark-clad figure enters. Bolts shoot across and both tense, waiting for a beating or a bullet, but to their relief, it's Jane.

"Don't speak – just listen," she whispers, "This purse holds enough money to get you tickets on the steamer to England. Go down to the bottom of the street, then hide yourselves in the lane there 'til it gets dark. I will come down with a carriage and get you to the boat – I know people down there who will make sure you get on – they owe me a favour. No time for questions now. Just go!"

The early sleet has stopped and the cold air forms a mist thick enough to hide the black mountain. They keep to the hedges and fences until they reach the dark welcome of the lane. Michan turns the fairy glass in his pocket and prays that the magic is still in it somewhere.

However, she has been dealt with; when Jane arrives with a carriage and horse, she seems bright-eyed and excited with her scheme. She explains that the child is very ill, and her parents – like many – blame the travellers for spreading diseases, refusing to listen to the fact that neither Kieran nor Michan has measles. Her cousin and husband believe the poor carry it in their clothing and touch. He would have had them arrested, but got caught up with obtaining the best doctor and medicines for his daughter, so Jane has managed to slip out to help them one last time.

In his mind, Michan sees Ailis and Ilene again, and wonders could a fine doctor have saved them too. As they reach the port, the crowds are still there, but their carriage is recognised and waved through, scattering groups settling for the night on their bundles and boxes. Jane buys them tickets and gives them the rest of the purse to keep. They cross the plank that leads up to the boat's deck, waving their thanks from the top.

As she turns to leave, she calls protection from the evil eye learned from Michan, "Blessings of God be upon you and all your labours," and slips away, melting into the crowds below.

Chapter 8

So, they step off the ancient land of the Tuatha, the land of great battles, of Finbarra and Oisin and the powerful Lugh Lamfada, all-wise and all knowledgeable. They are leaving behind the Sidhe in their caves and lakes, feasting forever and dancing to their too beautiful music.

They are each given a bunk in steerage class, which will fill up as the night goes on, but they have a little peace for a short while.

As they remove their boots to settle, Michan remembers, "I never told Jane the last story, Kieran – the one about Badh the Crow and her prophecy. She told it to Danu and her children." Kieran coughs quietly, but he listens.

"All life is transitory. Even our children are not immortal. The time will come when no one wants gods and goddesses to nurture them — when they are driven into darkness. A time approaches when the summer of Inisfail will be flowerless, when the cows shall be without milk. The seas will be without fish, the trees without fruit. There will be false and unjust laws, and honour will count for little. Warriors will betray each other and become thieves. There will come a time when there will be no more virtue left in this world."

Kieran coughs a while longer as they both drift into a

sad sleep. The rocking boat enables sleep, and down in steerage there is no idea of day or night. No storms come up, and all is steady until Michan wakes suddenly from a dream of a crow, which turns into a magpie and sings a song with beautiful words that he knows is not possible, even in his sleep. He wakes to find a pair of piercing eyes glaring at him in the gloom. It takes a moment to understand that what had seemed like feathers is actually the figure's rumpled hair.

"'Yer brother's ill – tis the fever – you need to get him out of here," a female voice hisses.

"We've all come this far – we want no fevers now," and a bony hand pulls at his bedding then gestures to the bunk below, holding a finger to her lips to keep him silent. He rolls off and leans into the bottom bed. Although he can see little, he hears the rolling rasp of Kieran's breath and feels the heat of his head. His stomach sinks. The other cabin members will turn on them if they think they've brought the fever in. Kieran might even be sent back to Eire. Thoughts of his body wrapped in a sheet and thrown deep into the Irish Sea flit through Michan's mind as he uses all his strength to half-walk, half drag him out to the central space where they had eaten earlier. Leaving him wrapped on the long bench, he goes back for their boots – they are not going to enter England barefoot. The ship's bell rings out the watch for six, so it must be morning. He uses a tin mug left lying there to take water from the barrel set nearby and props Kieran up to drink it. He moistens the edge of the thin blanket, pulled out with him from the bunk, and drips it on his head to try and cool him down. After a minute, his eyes fully open.

"I will get better," he says softly, then repeats as a question, "I will get better?"

"I have not wasted all this time on saving you, cara," Michan replies, though it was partly to save his own mortal, murdering soul that he had started. The ship is docking in a place called Heysham before sailing on to Liverpool, and Michan knows then they will have to disembark there, not wait for the big city. The cool water revives Kieran enough to put on his boots and sit up properly in time for the rest of the passengers arriving for their breakfast stirabout. Michan notices the woman who had entered their cabin giving them an encouraging nod as she passes. About midday, the boat's movement changes and a burly sailor comes down, shouting that all for Heysham should go aloft. A passenger calls the order again in Irish, and a few people begin to gather their packs and bags and move towards the steep stairway. Michan covers up Kieran's dizziness when he tries to stand by taking his arm and speaking clearly, "Come on, brother! We'll soon be home!"

The air on deck hits them with a cold hard punch. Grey skies promise chill rain, but to Michan's relief, there does not seem to be anyone checking passengers for health, which Joe Byrne had told them could happen. Groups of labourers stand by sizing up another boat load of immigrants who might be after their jobs. Few possessions and few with homes to go to. Then the hectic traffic of a working port takes over. The ship is taking on more coal to power it down to Liverpool, and goods are being disembarked and replaced with others. Michan and Kieran step off the wooden gangway and stand for a moment taking in the sights and smells of England. They manage to wander as convincingly as possible out of the gates and rest Kieran against a low wall. He has begun to shiver and mutter words that sound like 'win row win row' over and over. Enough of Jane's money remains to get them some food and warming beer from an inn nearby, and Michan manages to wake him enough to be placed on a bench at the back of the bar. The barman is friendly enough and sells him a shrub of rum and sugar for Kieran and a beer for himself, along with two pies of some unrecognisable meat. The first taste of his drink starts Kieran coughing again, but it wakes him up, and he drinks most of it, beginning to get his breath with each sup.

"We can find my aunt, the lady who Ma lived with when she fled Ireland. She will shelter us while I get better."

"But we lost the map long ago," Michan speaks through mouthfuls of both the pies, "How can we find her?"

"Da made me learn her address and name before we packed up and left. Maybe he knew death was coming?"

Michan closes his mind to the image of those eyes and the thrashing arms in the lake.   "Well, what is it?"

"Her name is Jessica Winrow – Ma's name – that's easy, and the place is called Ingleton."

"And?" asks Michan after a long pause.

"It's funny. We laughed about it when I was little, Da and I — Bank Bottom, 2 Bank Bottom! That's it – we can go there now!" Kieran is triumphant, and Michan is relieved.

Perhaps England would be kind to them, after all. Outside the inn, two or three carts wait for fares. An empty return journey tempts the carters to fill with anyone who will pay, and there's a good chance the drinkers inside are off a boat or steamer and in need of just such transport. Michan drags Kieran half over to the first in the row, hoping the driver thinks him drunk, not fevered. He is a small man with a huge leather belt holding up a pair of worn baggy trousers which run down to cracked leather boots, rivets striking the cobbles as he rounds the cart. His shadowed eyes are unseen beneath a wide-brimmed hat,

"How much you got lads?" He growls from a gap-toothed mouth.

Michan digs deep down, and his fingers briefly touch the fairy stone before he counts the coins there by shape and size. "Six pence, sir," he lies with innocent eyes.

"Turn out your pocket!" the carter growls again. He is in no hurry, and a fare for the journey to Ingleton would be an attractive bonus on a dull day. As Michan seems to hesitate and Kieran slips slowly to the ground, he pats the horse's rump and makes to mount the step to his seat on the cart, pausing to throw over his shoulder,

"I do not need to take you Irish urchins anywhere, and the extra cash I want is for feed for the horse, and my trouble, of course."

Michan can see no help around them, and reluctantly digs the last shilling from Jane out of his pocket and hands it over. The carter takes it almost lazily and tips his hat to them,

"It's Yates me name – Mr. Yates to you two – now get up quick!"

He sniffs and wipes his nose on his sleeve as Michan heaves Kieran up and covers them both with pungent straw. He is grateful that Kieran falls instantly into a deep sleep, and as they pull off and pick up the pace, he floats in and out of wakefulness to the clop of the horse's hooves. The steady rhythm lulls Michan into a half dream and the sound of the bodhran at those summer evening gatherings of his child-hood. A warm fire is crackling to the open sky, the drink flowing and women and men, freed from everyday life, taking their turns at sad and haunting songs, lively twisting dances with later tellings of the old stories. Tuatha and Sidhe are bat-tling and feasting behind the listener's dozing eyelids. Maybe it is Mr. Yates' worn boots and strong belt, but he can see clearly in his mind old Finn Cassidy, his Da's uncle, well away with the drink, his fire reddened hair sparking in the dark. He remembers strength and freedom in his childish body, tum-bling with his brothers through warm pockets between the adults and the fire. He can almost smell the beer, the poteen, and the smoke. Once, in a moment of silence, after Da had sung them all a lilting ballad, Patrick had caught him, and they had rolled to a stop at Finn's booted feet. He had belched loudly and laughed,

"Do not be lying there long lads, or the English will sell you away for meat!" Reckoning on the adults not caring much at that moment, he had sat up and asked the question often on his mind, "How does the land belong to anyone? Is it not just there – beneath our feet?"

Old Finn had sucked a little more on his poteen, then pronounced, "They come and lay their gold down upon it, Michan. It makes a wide golden path stretching away to the sea both ways, and then it is their own." He had pulled himself up straight and stretched his arms out to each side to illus-trate his point, and Da had exclaimed,

"Would you look at Finn now – he thinks he's Jesus!"

and the moment broke as everyone had begun to laugh and point. The next day and for many more, he had searched for it, the golden road, but like the fairy rath, his eye had never caught it. Finn Cassidy had gone off to build the government roads when the hunger got worse, and Michan never saw him again, although he had always hoped he'd found some of the gold.

The evening closes in as they reach Ingleton after one stop midway, and they sit up to take in the place. Kieran has improved after his long sleep, and Mr. Yates puts them out just before the bridge into the town and the first row of stone houses leading downhill to the centre. A child near an inn tells them the way to Bank Bottom, and in moments they are there. The noise of a river close by bubbles over a stony bed, and in front of it, a row of neat cottages hug its banks, their slate rooves and regular windows facing the lane. Lamps are already burning in number two, throwing moving shapes behind them in the rooms beyond.

Kieran steps up to the door and knocks. It opens slowly, and a woman's face and hand appear, shadowed in the light of a swinging lantern.

"Yes?" she asks, her voice firm and young.

With an effort to control the coughing fit that now takes him, Kieran splutters between gasps, "My name is Kieran Quinn, my mother was Elizabeth Winrow, my father, Edward Quinn. I need to see my aunt Jessica now."

The door opens suddenly wide, and an older plump and bespectacled woman peers out. She pushes forward and snatches the lamp from the door opener's hand, holding it up to scrutinise Kieran's face. After what seems like a long moment, she breaks into a smile and follows it with a sob,

"Little Kieran! She talked of you so much – she knew you would come one day. The last of her babies left!" He finds his breath cut off by strong arms, and the coughing doubles through him as she pulls him inside. He doesn't hear the words muttered above its sound, but Michan, hanging back in the shadows, does.

"Those feckless Irish – they took no care, your father's people – all the same – now look at the mess they've made for themselves!"

He shrinks back further and hears the front door close with a decisive click. He watches the movement through the windows for a while, then steps forward and knocks, but no one answers him.

All around darkness falls, and the evening cold draws in. Finally, the shutters at an upstairs window are closed tight, and the other lights go out. He knows he should be glad that Kieran is safe, but the dark quiet of the night feels empty. Taking out the fairy stone, he holds it up to the newly rising moon and lets its perfect colour fill his view. He has been here before. He will find a place to stay and come back in the daylight to see Kieran again. Crossing himself against the evil eye, he turns and heads down the lane to search for a barn, a cave, or maybe a stable warmed by its sleeping occupant. Tomorrow is always better.

Chapter 9

The next day breaks bright through the beams of the barn he has found. For a moment, he remembers nothing. Then reality jolts him as a rough voice shouts,

"You can come down from there right now – don't try to run – I'm bigger and stronger than most!"

With a sinking feeling, he knows the game is up and starts to descend the hayloft ladder, jumping the last three rungs and landing at the feet of a giant. His brown boots are the first thing confronting Michan; then his eyes travel up over a long woollen coat tied with a rope to a flat cap with a peak perching above a mop of curly greying hair and a thick black beard.

"So – tell me what you're doing here, though I can guess by the look of you!" the man booms in an amiable enough tone, and Michan pulls himself up to his full height, reaching only to the man's chest.

"I needed a place to sleep," he replies in clear English, "I did no harm and will be gone now," he pleads as he makes a dive for the barn door. Suddenly, his feet fly through the air as the man grabs his coat, lifting him like a new-born kitten.

"Oh no you don't!" the giant laughs in a deep rumble. "You owe me for a night's board. Now let's decide how you can pay. Sit here on that bale so that we can sort it out." He drops Michan hard upon it.

'Sometimes the world, or perhaps the fairies, throw some good his way', is Michan's thought as he makes the acquaintance of Joshua Wallwork, farmer. He needs some labouring help around his property. His son has gone to work in the mine in Ingleton, and both his daughters and their husbands work in the mill. The farmer's offer of paid work seems almost too good to be true. Wallwork knows little of Jessica Winrow but will allow Michan to visit his friend when his jobs for the day are done.

From that moment, life develops a pattern for Michan. Every day he goes about labouring, building, mending, and tending to Joshua's livestock, and in the evenings, he walks down to the row of little houses beside the river to call for Kieran. Each time, the servant answers and tells him to leave and that Mr. Quinn is ill and does not want to see him. So, life goes around in circles. He is well fed at the farm, and building strength and muscle with the work there, and Joshua and his family are becoming friends. He talks to them of his home, the Maguires, and his long journey to England. They listen but seem to find it difficult to believe— or that Kieran exists. To his delight, he has been given a real bed in an outbuilding that was once part of the dairy. He often lies awake at night, finding stories in his head to tell an imaginary Kieran and his brothers and Ilene, all perched on the low byre wall beside the bed. One night he reminds them of the Tuatha de Danaan and their great skills in magic and necromancy. They all lean closer to hear him better.

"A fearful, fighting race called the Milesians were going

to conquer the Tuatha completely, but they became fascinated and captivated by those gifts and the power they gave the Tuatha, and they allowed them to remain in Eire and build forts. There the Milesians held parties with music and singing and the chant of bards. They bred their magnificent horses in the caves of the hills where they lived and rode them about mounted all by the sons of kings with gold helmets and golden spears in their hands. So, they lived for a hundred years or more, for by their enchantments they could resist death."

At those last words, his listeners vanish and for a while he repeats the phrase for them, as if the chant might somehow still hold power,

"Resist death, resist death, resist death."

The next day when he has finished his work, he heads again down to Bank Bottom as usual. He knows the village by now, and people even nod to him when they pass. Miss Winrow's maid, Mary, walks his way to visit her mother on her half-day free, and he has decided to gain her confidence. She always wants to prattle of injustices, imagined or not, and gossip of village life, and he pretends an interest without mentioning Kieran, although she still waves him goodbye cheerily with,

"He's no better – she'll not let you in," and strides off up the hill past the farm. This day though, she hurries up when she sees him,

"They can't fix him now – he's really bad. Almost gone!"

For a moment, everything stops, and her 'Goodbye then' rings in his ears as she moves quickly on. In her mind, there's nothing she can do, and this one might be ill too for all she knows.

"No – wait!" Michan almost yells," and pounds after her. "You can let me in, Mary – please let me in! I have to say good-bye – I have to tell him something!"

Stopped in her tracks by the hint of gossip to come, she turns and waits.

"I'm on my half-day – I can't go back now! But I could let you in tomorrow. She's always out to the shops between eight and nine of the morning. If you come to the back by the river, I'll leave the door unlocked. He's up the stairs on the right – though it might be a corpse by then, of course! And you have to tell me your secret first, or I won't do it!" she smiles sweetly and adopts what she feels is a questioning pose, tapping her boot rhythmically and leaning her bonneted head to one side.

For a moment, Michan is lost for words, and then the idea comes to him out of the blue,

"She's his real mother. His Da told me when he was dying. He said he loved Miss Winrow first and deepest, but the scandal was too much, so they took the baby with them to Ireland when he married."

"Eeeh!" Mary whistles on a long breath out, "She never did, and her so holy too!"

"So now will you keep your side of the bargain? You can tell everyone after I've told him first – but not before." Michan is becoming more and more insistent as the agony of keeping the girl sweet is tearing him apart. He wants to shout and shake her. "You will be my friend in our secret un-til then?" he coaxes, in the way his younger brothers and Ilene had taught him. To his relief, she relaxes and gives him an exaggerated wink, placing her finger on her lips with a giggle.

"Tomorrow then," she agrees, before setting off towards her mother's house again. Michan tumbles into the hedge muttering 'Resist death' over and over as he pulls weeds from the wayside grasses.

The night drags along sleepless, and Michan starts early on the tasks Joshua has given him so that he can get away for half an hour at eight o clock, missing the hot breakfast that they all share after finishing the first jobs of the day. The river bubbles along the shallow stone bed behind Bank Bottom, and a muddy path skirts the walls of the little gardens. No one is around, although the usual noise from a working mill fills the air. The latch on the door lifts smoothly, and he treads softly up the narrow wooden stair. Stuffy air gets thicker as he opens the door that Mary had pointed out. Inside, the shutters are closed, and he has to squint to get used to the light. A rasping gasping sound leads him to the bed and tells him that Kieran still lives.

"Kieran, cara," he mutters quietly and feels the power of sharing in their language again.

"Michan! It's you! I must be bad then!"

"No! I tried to come so much, but that old witch would not let me in. I even threw stones at your window, but she threatened to send Mary for the constable. We had enough of them, didn't we?"

"Aye, we did – in Ireland. But how are you feeling now? Do you fancy coming out on the road with me again?" The breathing sounds seem to slow and become a little calmer then.

"No cara – I am too soft now with this comfortable bed. I will stay here and rest a bit more." The voice, almost too quiet to hear, fills Michan with a shaft of pain.

He knows he has to tell him the truth, the reason why he came. "You know she's not your mother." He chuckles, guessing that Mary could not have kept it to herself.

"Of course, I know! A good story, though! One of your best." Michan can hear the smile in his voice.

The rasping seems to ease off even further, and in the almost silence, Michan takes a breath and launches into the story he needs to tell. "I'm sorry, Kieran – your Da – he didn't give me his coat and shoes. He didn't die a peaceful death. I pushed him into the lake, and I didn't try to save him even though I could have. I watched him die."

His voice trails off then as he realises that the rasping sound has stopped, his confession not heard. Kieran has gone. Michan does not know how long he sits in the gloomy room, but time seems to stretch and shrink until a noise downstairs heralds the return of Miss Winrow and breaks the spell. He jumps up and throws open the shutters and windows on both sides. In the new streaming daylight, he turns to Kieran, thin and pale, eyes open, a question lingering in them. He touches the cooling hand, resting on the coverlet for the healing power it can give. Gently closing the eyes, he mutters in the language they shared,

"Teigh anois... go now. Go dance with the Sidhe, cara," and then turns to leave the room.   Pushing past the fussing women on the stairs, he clatters out into the street where the day goes on in its normal rhythms – the river gurgles and splashes, the mill clatters, and a smell of spring begins to carry on the air.

Back at the farm, the days become busier, and Michan throws himself into every task he is given. The servant, Mary, had come to speak to Joshua a few days after Kieran's death, and he is allowed to go up the hill to the graveyard behind the old church for the funeral. Arriving early, he finds the gravedigger shoulder-deep in his job. The man lets him look at the black stone above the grave, and he asks him what it says. He cannot read either but has memorised all the headstones he works beside.

"This one's for the Winrow family," he explains between gulps of beer from a stone jar. "It says: Thomas Winrow—his wife Sarah—daughter Elizabeth," pointing to each name as he repeats it, "Elizabeth, she's the latest in here, only a year hence. There was talk she took her own life—died by her own hand so to speak. She fell when out walking at Beezley Falls, slipped on the wet moss up there. Who knows, or even cares?" He shrugs philosophically. "This one coming's her son anyhow. Escaped from that wild country Ireland where his father had taken them. Wonder if *he* lives – and where he was buried?" Finally, he places the jug on the growing pile of earth beside him and sets to digging with a grunt.

Michan steps backward with a shiver and, scrambling up, finds himself facing Jessica Winrow, an angry black taffeta ball rolling towards the grave.

"You – leave at once! You are trespassing! That grave is my family's property! I should have had you arrested when you broke into my house!" she spits at him. A solemnly decorated cart has pulled up behind her, and the undertaker's men are unloading a simple wooden coffin.

"I hope you may enjoy your family's property soon, madam!" he says as she reaches him.

A black-robed priest is heading swiftly towards them from the church. For a moment, Michan seizes the chance to place his hand on the head of the coffin giving Kieran the honour which tradition demands. Then he walks off with as much dignity as he can muster, winking at Mary with the quip,

"Black suits you, cara!"

He does not look back.

Chapter 10

Remembering wakes from those days, when people sat up all night, sometimes wailing and telling long tales of good about the dead, punctuating these with drafts of whisky to see the person on his or her way, he finds himself entering the inn near the bridge. Inside, it is a typical day. A few miners not on shift, and a couple of older men with sticks surround the small tables. A fire crackles in the grate even though the day is warm.

His first two whiskies are for Kieran and his father, then another for poor Sarah in her slippery fall. By the time he is toasting Ailis and his younger brothers, he doesn't feel the burn and finds his speech has become so eloquent that everyone should hear what he has to say.

"'Tis a wake," he starts, giving forth to the newly attentive company, "Me friend is dead. All me family too. Ma and all me brothers and sisters and his Da too – I killed the Da mind— and his mother slipped by a waterfall — or maybe didn't slip?" This question suddenly seems very funny, and he starts to giggle.

"That's enough, lad!" the publican cuts him off as another man steps forward.

"Take your lies out of here – you Irish are all drunks!" he shouts.

It's now the black mist comes over him for the first time. He does not even feel his knuckles hitting the bone and flesh as both men fall to the floor— Michan's fists punching again and again until strong arms wrestle him up and pin him tight, helping his opponent's blows carve up his face until he forgets everything. Later, when he wakes, every bit of him aches, and the contents of his stomach just manage to hit the bucket he finds beside him. He lifts his head and through swollen eyes, squints at the bars of what seems to be a cage of some sort.

A voice, quite close, chuckles, "Bet that feels better, son!" One swollen eye opens enough to allow the image of a very tall man to form, his boots almost as shiny as the row of buttons running down his coat front. Michan struggles upright and takes in that this is a policeman, and he is in the town lock-up.

There are moments when life takes a path, whether chosen or not, and through all his aching bruised flesh, he knows this is another to add to his journey. The officer stands in front of him, idly tapping his stick against the opposite palm. He is poised like a farm cat before a hole in the barn wall. Then he turns to his desk and pours out some liquid from a jug into a tin mug and holding it out, asks, "Thirsty, are you? Get up and come over here."

Michan creaks to a standing position and, when his dizziness has passed, realises that the lock-up is only as big as a cottier's living space, and two steps allow him to steady himself on the bars. The water hits him hard in the face, and he gasps for air as he staggers back onto the bed, every bruise screaming out for notice. As he splutters and chokes, the officer shakes with laughter and pours another cup. He places it safely on the floor just inside the bars, chuckling, "Here – what a mess you've made! Just drink it, man," then sinks onto his twisting chair.

Woken up by the drenching, Michan grabs the cup and gulps it all down greedily. He has no idea what is to happen, but part of him remembers the satisfaction of the release of anger at the inn, and he decides not to say anything for now, having no desire to feed the cruelty of this man. The officer then pretends to write and ignore him, occasionally muttering as if reading, 'Mmm – two months hard labour', or 'Six weeks on the treadmill if you're lucky', and 'solitary confinement at least', until the heavy nailed door swings open and Joshua Wallwork steps inside. His bulk fills the room, and his voice sets off Michan's headache again.

"Morning, brother," he nods to the officer, then takes in the state of Michan. "Oh man – they took their punishment out on you good and proper! So, what are we going to do with him, John?"

"It's all prepared, Joshua – you make your mark here, and you can have him – but he has to move on. That's the arrangement she made – you know..."

"Aye John – he'll move – we'll see to that. T'was the agreement – Miss Winrow was generous with the fine payment though, eh?"

"A kind and generous lady indeed," Joshua's brother comments as he stands and rattles a bunch of large keys, choosing the biggest to slide into the black lock on the bars.

They swing open, easily providing enough room for him to reach in and pull Michan up by the collar, heaving him towards the still-open front door.

The two brothers' farewells filling his ears, Michan finds himself standing shakily on the cobbles in front of the farm cart. The journey back passes in silence through Bank Bottom, where Michan is almost certain he glimpses Mary's hand waving from the front window, until they turn rattling into the farm track. Inside, Joshua drops Michan at his dairy sleeping space and tells him to stay there until sent to come in for the last supper with the family. Once the farmer has gone, Michan slips down under his blankets and slides into a dreamless sleep. Waking when the dark is falling, he finds one of Joshua's daughters standing beside him, a cup in her hand. For a moment he flinches, but she smiles through the twilight, "Here – it's a drink with feverfew to ease the pain. Da says to come and eat now", and to his surprise, he is hungry.

The big table fills the warm kitchen, its well-stocked top of stew and potatoes ringed by all the family. As usual, they eat in silence, then when all has been cleared, Joshua speaks.   "As we all know, Michan here has got himself into trouble. Miss Winrow paid for his release, but for that, he has to move on." This news is greeted by protests from his daughters and sons in law and a triumphant gasp from his son.

"Tis only right – I saw what he did to Adam Harris!"

"Enough, Seth – they took their revenge as you can see."

Joshua points in Michan's direction, "Tomorrow, you must move on man. I will miss your good work — but I cannot keep you here. Do you have anywhere you can go at all?"

Michan's voice cracks as he replies uncertainly, "There's a

cousin of my Da – he lives in a place called Durham. I could look for him."

"There are mines there," says Seth, "You could find work easily."

"Aye, his family told us he got work in the mines there – if I find him, I could join him." A small hope is lit in Michan somehow. He could find a home there with a real family, perhaps even make his own home, his own new family.

The next day, dawn finds him loaded with a bag of food for the journey and money in his pocket for a room each night, his stomach full with the comfort of a Wallwork breakfast. He reaches the road and faces the direction Joshua pointed out to him. His bruises are beginning to settle into purples and yellows, but the dark inside still churns as his boots set into a steady eastward tread. The day is bright and the path is not much frequented. Air blows freshly around him, and his heart eases a little with the sound of the long-beaked curlews calling to each other as they leap from cover and arc above, speckled brown bodies a flash against the gorse. There are no mountains or even drumlins, but strange grey rock shapes rise like platforms set for a train to stop. Later he watches two lapwings dance around each other, their pointed head feathers proud to the sky even as they move, black collars above white chests flashing and turning. For a moment, he thinks to find their nest and take the eggs but remembers he has food this time and money — there is no need to scavenge. He has no idea of time except by the sun's movement, and when it seems to be a little after mid-day, he sits to eat his lunch.

All around, he recognises the new-born flowers of wild

thyme, violet and purple, the yellow and white of rock rose and hawkweed, and even fairy flax. He tries to concentrate on the fact that its seeds can cause flux and sickness. Still, the thought keeps bringing him back to Ireland and finding the drooping heads and narrow leaves for Ailis to use as medicine, searching across the gorse with his brothers, to add it to the yellow hawkweed that they had collected for colds and chest problems. Then he sees her clearly showing Ilene how to prepare the flowers to make a medicine, leaning her dark head down to reach the bright white one, then standing up to face him, green eyes sparkling with thanks for his basket as her free hand reaches to ruffle his hair. His own hand reaches up to touch hers before the image breaks, and she is gone. Michan pulls the warm coat that Joshua gave him for the journey around him and lays back upon the rock. He has been walking since dawn, and the food and beer make him drowsy. Placing his money safely in his boot, he allows himself to drift off.

Ailis is sitting on the straw in their hut in the dream that comes. Da is to one side, and Ilene on her knee. She tells them the story of where the knowledge of herbs for healing came from in the early days of long ago. Outside, the wind is blowing up, rattling through the roof, and the pig snores softly by the fire.

"Now the Tuatha-de-Danaan had a great knowledge of the powers of herbs," she begins, "and this led them to be known as sorcerers and necromancers. There was a battle at a place called Moytura in County Mayo —oh, it was about three thousand years ago — and a wise priest or druid was the doctor to the army of the Tuatha. He prepared a bath of herbs and plants near the battleground, and all the wounded who plunged into it came out completely healed of all their injuries —except one! The king at the time called Nuad had lost his hand, and the bath had no power to heal this, so the wise druid made him a silver hand."

He hears again his family's collective gasp at this strange image.

"Nothing is left to tell us how they fixed it to his arm, but it must have worked and the king was ever after known as Nuad of the Silver Hand!"

He wakes with the call of a lapwing close to his ear and jumps up, shaking the dream away with his head. He would like to be back to that time when all seemed so clear, and nothing could go wrong. His fingers stiff with sleep, not silver, untie his bootlace and take the money out, slipping it back into an inner coat pocket. He looks towards the track which crosses the moor, and sees a few more travellers on the way now. His head feels calmer, as if the thought of herbs alone has taken away the pain. As he sets off again, he smiles to himself at the memory of Sean and Pol playing at gluing a hand one onto the other and waving it stiffly at Ilene, until she ran inside and hid with her pig. Back on the track, he falls in with two countrymen heading northeast to the mines as well, and they pass the time with talk of home until, around sunset, they reach an inn nestling in a dip and decide to take a room and a meal. Inside, the place is more welcoming than it had looked from outside.

After eating, Michan rolls himself in a rough blanket on a straw mattress in a shared room and drifts off to the comforting snores around him and an image of Ilene's pig.

Part 2

1875

ENGLAND

Chapter 1

Sometimes it feels to Michan that the years seem to have hurtled by but also dragged at a snail's pace. He is still walking.

The looming black shapes of industry roll out across the landscape behind him as the mines begin to fade into the background, and the fells spread out before his feet. A railway line snakes away in the distance with now and again a plume of white chasing it along. He walks determinedly, each step measured, only pausing to cough now and again. Today, he heads as far away from the mines as he can get on foot, leaving behind the grey cindered air and the darkness. This place has been his home for twenty eight years now, and he knows in many ways it saved him. Sometimes, however, he feels that he must have angered a Púca, and even though his life has many blessings, it still crouches inside him, demanding to be fed. A spirit of good or bad — perhaps they had forgotten to leave the stalks for it that last good harvest before the hunger came, and its anger was his punishment.

Michan enjoys the comfort of his walking boots, which are much softer than his work ones, and the fact that he can walk out here on the fell in them. He listens for merlin and curlew calls and looks out for the rare sight of pearl, orange, and green butterflies or the rustle of a timid adder in the spiked heather. Today in late summer, no ice-fingered wind blows up, and the sun scuds in and out of clouds on a gentle breeze. This path is the way he had come all those years ago from Ingleton, Joshua Wallwork's money a weight in his pocket and no clue where to start looking for his cousin, Liam Donegan, and a possible home.

His journey had prepared him for those few weeks hiding in sheds and the shelter of hedges so he could save his money for food. To his relief, he had met the groups of Irish around the Durham villages. They always seemed to know someone who knew someone who had met the Donegan family— until he tracked them down at last.

He felt he had found a welcome then and John had got him his first work in the mine. His memory carries him back to that first time going inbye at the mine at Felling with Liam, his Da, and little brother. A wrap of bread and cheese in one hand and pick over his shoulder, he'd squashed up in the cage, Ailis' voice whispering in his mind of the Sidhe maidens who could influence a man to commit any crime from their dark vaults here beneath the earth. He smiles as he remembers crossing himself as he stepped out at the bottom and young Ralph Donegan had nudged him,

"It's alright, Michan —there's nothing left to take —we've had all the fairy gold and diamonds already!" All the Irish around had laughed at the lad's words.

The back-breaking work crawling down three foot high tunnels, bursting out into wood-framed vaults, and the fear of fire damp always there, had at least meant that he had some money to pay for lodgings in the Donegan's roof bedroom.

Four years of this had fled by somehow, although when the boiler explosion killed little Ralph, the anger awoke again inside him and the drinking and fighting returned.

Michan stops then to listen to a bubbling stream and a peewit's call as it circles high above it. At that time, it had been Mary who saved him. He thinks of her now, rounded and work hardened, little Kieran born late to her, and then remembers his first sight—golden-red curls and bright blue eyes whose glance caused sparks of desire to flicker through his body. He pauses to cough for a while—the collier's curse—then finds a clearing to sit and pull out the meal she has given him. Looking up, he allows the soft sun to warm his face. Its touch brings back the memory of the tear tracks down Bridget Donegan's face when John brought her the news of little Ralph's death—blown to a thousand pieces by the exploding pit head boiler. John had to see him —claim what was left of his body. She had sobbed,

"It might not be him, John—not him!" But it was.

Taking a swig of the beer, he remembers it was then that he began the drinking and fighting in earnest again. Within a year, he'd been turned out by his only family and found a place in a boarding house—a widow renting to single miners as her men were all gone. Another year and twice more he was arrested, the luck of his blue stone freeing him both times. The widow's angry face as she threw his bag at him made him smile now — though it hadn't then. So, he had walked again. This time to Cassop—hoping no one had heard his story.

The gasp of a distant train comes and goes as he packs up his sack and heads a little further across the empty land.

Smiling to himself, he remembers the saving that came with that move. Lodgings with the Fitzpatrick family, his wife, and the two daughters left at home shine a happy light on that part of his past. Mary was the youngest, and long walks together when shifts permitted soon led to Thomas's creation and a hasty wedding. Those Bond day moves when every April a miner had to sign a new contract and sell himself body and soul to another pit owner. Moving pits, he had to hope that the house they got was neither wringing in damp nor shared with the black carapaces of scuttering cockroaches. Mary had always settled their growing family as best she could, building a warm hearth and scrubbing the places clean as soon as they had put in the few sticks of furniture they owned. A room full of babies and children had seemed to turn so quickly into their life now. Thomas and Sean are grown men and miners themselves, Ailis and Peig away and married to miners, one a mother herself too.

Life should be calmer — but that Púca of anger still writhes inside him. Old Finn's path of gold stretches yet across Ireland and all the northern coalfields. He knows the only small power he has is to support independence from afar, and the Fenians seem to be the only way to do this – even though there is a doubt beginning to seed itself somewhere in his mind. Stories of The Brotherhood had made sense to him in those young and vigorous days. In those days, meeting together in the pub on a Saturday evening, before the one generous day of rest, to share stories of hunger and exile, had fuelled all their anger. To overthrow the government that had led to such destruction in his country seemed the right thing to attempt back then – though he happily went back to work with his English marrers on the Monday shift.

It still surprises him that, somehow, he has risen to be the leader of this local group. He knows there is a signal coming, and when it does, his group is ready to breach a gap in that path of gold. He already has a message from Newcastle; McMahon and Walsh will be down to stiffen his resolve—they want no wavering about whether anyone will be killed or injured and have heard rumours about his possible weakness. However angry he still is, Michan hopes that he will miss them today if he takes his time —Thomas and Sean can organise it; their youth gives them that determination which his age begins to lack.

A coughing bout wrenches him again, and he has to pause. When he straightens up, he sees the ruin of a house just ahead, its dry-stone garden wall still sturdy, its doors and windows gaping black. He sits on the wall to rest for a moment, unhooking his pack and resting it at his feet. Closing his eyes, he allows his breath to return to normal and feels the sun gentle on the back of his head. When he opens them again, he sees a little way away what seems to be a white bird like a swan flapping and twisting around, then in a blink, it becomes a little girl dancing.

"Hello!" he calls out, but she doesn't seem to hear and skips off, giggling, around the side of the house. Michan's heart sinks as he knows he can't just leave her— she could be lost— unless someone is living in the blind, yawning building. Reluctantly he picks up his pack and sets off after the little figure, when a voice stops him,

"' Tis good that wall can hold you up!"

He turns to find a person just behind him. He thinks it must be a woman from the shawl though the voice is as deep as a man's. She is sucking on a long clay pipe, and her face is as wrinkled as a naked baby bird.

"Good day to you, sir," she says next. "Come away in for you need a sit and a rest from the sound of that cough." She gestures with the pipe, and he finds himself following her into the open mouth of the house. Inside it is dark, but even though the grate is cold, it feels quite warm. She sits them down in two ragged chairs in front of the hearth and leans back, "Now then, how can I help you?" she asks as if he had made the journey purposely to see her.

"Where is the little girl?" he manages, overcoming his astonishment. She takes three more slow puffs on the pipe and clears her throat ignoring his question. Silence grows around them for a while. Eventually, she says, "What is making you so angry then, sir? That is easier to answer, is it not?"

He begins to speak before he forms a thought, "I cannot forgive myself for killing a man. I could have saved him. Also, for never letting his son know the truth of it." The words surprise him as he had not thought of the dead man in the lake for many years.

"You were no more than a child then — you must forgive the child. Is the son dead too?" she asks. He nods.

"Then he knows — or if he knows nothing tis all the same. The anger is deeper than that, Sir. I feel it is."

"I'm tired," he sighs, "but I can't forgive so easily, woman—it twists in me this anger!"

He feels it begin to grow again; his starving family dying one by one, cottages burning on a hillside, the workhouse grave pits, drunken fights, violent policemen, Kieran's grave, a child blown to pieces, and his heavy-hearted walk from Ingleton. To his horror, he finds himself crying, great sobs wracking his body until they turn into coughs, almost thrusting him out of the chair. When it's over, he thinks she may have gone like a fairy wraith, but she is still there, filling the clay pipe thoughtfully.

"And what about the Fenians?" she asks and waits.

His first reaction, when asked about them, is always denial. No one must know who the members are for everyone's safety. "What do you know of them?" he asks and is surprised by her deep-throated laugh.

"I know you know," she chuckles, "What is it they want you to do now? Blow something up? Tell me what is right in your life – what gives you reason to live above the anger?"

So, he tells her of Mary, his strong sons, three loving daughters, and the extra gift of little Kieran. Of the beautiful stories of his mother Ailis, the Tuatha, regular food, friends and a warm place to sleep. Suddenly he realises that there is something he must do.

"That's it!" she says from the folds of the chair even though he hasn't spoken, "You know what to do now. What to keep, what to change, what to set free. Go home now, Michan – it's getting late."

Before he can ask her how she knows his name, he hears the little girl giggling again and turns to look through the glassless window.

"Look, I was right, she's out there, look!" and he points to show the woman, but when he turns back, she is gone. The shape of her rests in the chair, and the smell of pipe smoke lingers, but somehow he knows that even if he searches for her everywhere, she will be gone.

The dark has come down when he finally reaches Cornsay Colliery again, but he feels lighter. Even the ash and cinders glittering through the gaslight do not trouble him. He strolls home, not wanting to run into McMahon and Walsh again. They had to return to Newcastle last night, and he has the instructions for the pick up at Esh Winning station. He will be on shift when they return tomorrow. That will give him an extra day before any signal can be sent, and he hopes to deflect it before Thomas, Sean, and the rest of the cell realise it ever arrived.

Mary is already asleep in the press bed. The kitchen table is pushed back, and Kieran sleeps in his wooden cradle beside her. She mumbles something, but he can't make it out, so he ladles a bowl of cold stew from the iron pot on the range and chews it as quietly as he can before pulling off his boots and clothes and taking his nightshirt from the rack where it is warming. Then climbing under the heavy bed-spread, he rolls down the well-worn mattress hill towards her, wrapping his arm around her comforting body.

He vaguely wonders as he drifts off where Ina is—her bed in the front parlour has not been slept in. She will have to stop visiting her sister Ailis so often, now the second child is coming.

Chapter 2

Looking back, I see that my life really began with that journey. Every clack of the rails, each puff of cinder ridden smoke flying past the carriage window, told me I was on my way. Life was calling me at last. Twenty one years of everyday tedium grew more distant with each yard we travelled.

I leaned back against the rough cloth of the upright seat and sang in my head, 'I'm really leaving, I've really left', in time with the iron wheels. The map crackled comfortably in my pocket whenever I moved, and I must have drifted off for a while. I was back in the vicarage gazing out of the nursery window; I had never been allowed my own adult room and especially not my brother's room — the empty shrine. The path down to the village lay white in the moonlight. Coming along it towards me in his glamorous uniform, brass buttons glinting but drained of scarlet, came Will—my hero brother. He walked jauntily, although I knew he was dead, and I did not want him to reach the house. Then, suddenly, he was in front of my window, his skull picked clean, coat hanging on a frame of bones and my own voice was shouting, 'Go away– Go away!'

I woke to my pounding heart and the twilit compartment. The bowler-hatted man opposite shook his newspaper and tutted loudly and the woman to my right pulled her child closer to her and turned pointedly away. For a while I could not shake the dread feeling of that dream, so I tried to replace Will's death with thoughts of happier times in Ely and Prickwillow. Miss Doggett's day school floated into my mind and brought me some comfort. Walking along holding Bridie's hand through the busy streets of Ely everything had seemed full of colour and movement; people bustling about, voices calling, the clattering of horses' hooves on the cobbles, smells from the market, spices, herbs, fruit and the sweetness of bloody meat hanging in rows; Bridie's hand in mine feeling warm, not cold like Mother's; Miss Doggett, round and comfortable in her too large flopping bonnet, smiling at the front door of the house that seemed to lean over, as if needing to be held up by the one opposite; the dark wood framing white clay walls and metal mullioned windows; learning letters and numbers with three other boys at a parlour table, and sometimes with Will before he went away to school. Mrs Doggett was always kind to us, and to Mother and Father's surprise, sparing the rod actually helped us learn.

The rattle of the train wheels seemed to me then to push time on with them and those fractured memories that crowd the brain when half asleep stepped forward for attention. The doctor —his top hat making him seem like a giant to my seven year old self —talking over my head as if I was invisible, telling my father that, since the accident, I would always have the problem of one leg shorter than the other and as I seemed to be delicate, I should be kept at home, not sent away like Will. Those long days in the vicarage at Prickwillow, Will only visiting in the holidays. The excitement of the nursery's new occupant; that little bundle, fair curls and brown eyes peeping out from a blanket, the comfort it gave me telling her long stories even though she couldn't know what I was saying, myself her only visitor for hours. Even as a new-born, Etta seemed to know that she was an extra in the family— pleasant to look at but of little worth, about the same as me–the limping child–the twin who should have died. Gradually the memory of sunlight on the riverbanks led me away from those darker places. Bridie taking us, with Etta, when she was a little older, in the carriage down to the river. It had seemed as if the sun always shone on those days, and I stretched, finding myself smiling around the occupants of the rocking railway compartment although they were mostly dozing by then or avoiding my gaze.

My hip and knee ached after such a long time in one place and I moved into a more comfortable position using my coat as a pillow against the cold glass of the windowpane. As I closed my eyes and tried to sleep the riverbank and the sunshine returned. Those games we played with the children there, John Hill from the farm and his two cousins Ned and Jim; I could see them clearly, Jim a little older than us and the other two tousle haired and brown from the sun. All of us looking after Etta when she could walk, while Bridie dozed on the grass. Those times we even went down into the river, the water ice cold after the sun on the bank. Ned and Jim trying to teach me to swim, while John slid backwards and forwards like a rippling pink fish. The feeling of Bridie rubbing me roughly down with my dry shirt then smuggling us up the back stairs so mother would not find out what I had been doing.

Memories of the cool dark in the nursery took over then— rolling about in the burning itch of measles, chicken pox, scarlet fever and the aching throat of mumps. The only visitor allowed at those times was Bridie with broth and poultices, and sometimes, if I begged her, beautiful stories of magic people, journeys and feasts, and gentle sad songs in her own language. Mother never came near. Before I could block it I was older, outside Father's study hearing the raised voices of both my parents.

"Calm yourself Ann!" came in a cold tone from my father, followed by mother in full flow,

"No, tell me Charles, what gift are those children from your God? A crippled useless boy and a girl? A perfect twin taken instead of him, and only one son of any worth left to us to thank Him for. Tell me!"

The colours of the floor tiles spun past me again in my memory and not knowing how I got there, I found myself in the pantry–my hiding place. I sank down on a sack of flour and cried great wracking sobs until a thought began to gradually take shape,

"I am not useless–I am not useless–I will show her!" and finally I drifted off to sleep.

The next time I jolted awake a guard was shouting, "Anyone for Darlington–this stop Darlington." I grabbed my bag from the rack and queued behind the man with the newspaper and the now whingeing child and its mother, and we stepped down into a cloud of smoke. I had arrived.

The flat station roof above me seemed to float on clouds of steam. Even at that early hour of the morning people were rushing in and out of the fog it created. As the train pulled out on its way to Scotland the smoke lifted, and gaslights showed my way to a waiting room and the men's lavatory. There was no one there, so I opened my case and found my small bottle of Macassar oil, applying a few drops to revive my combed down hair and reshape my moustache. A glance in the worn thin mirror showed it still held its pointed shape and my cravat was tucked neatly into my waistcoat. I had worn a sack coat to travel and smoothed it down as best I could before putting on the overcoat that Bridie had insisted I bring for the northern weather. It was too early to try and find the newspaper office so I made myself comfortable in the waiting room on an empty bench. Using my valise as a pillow I managed a couple more hours of sleep before an irate gentleman knocked my feet and demanded that I move so that he could sit down.

By then the day seemed to be a little lighter, so straightening myself up, I picked up my luggage and set off for the exit, heading over a wooden bridge and down into the street. The mud of the road sucked and slipped around my shoes and everywhere faces emerged through the smoky grey haze, then disappeared just as suddenly. I took my watch from its pocket to check the exact time as there was no way to tell through the fog whether I was early or late. Maps are little use when you can't make out street names or turnings and I was beginning to cough. Mother's waspish voice came back to me then, 'Well Thadeus – I did warn you! The town is not the country, and especially one in the North!'

Eventually, after narrowly avoiding the fourth cart that thundered up out of the gloom, I found myself on a bridge, the ground becoming firmer as my spirits lifted. There was a bridge on the map over a wide river–I must've been in the right place! At that point, daylight seemed to be gradually breaking through and a cobbled square spread out in front of me bordered by a market. The usual headless animal corpses hung in rows to one side, their ribs shining pale against red flesh. Beyond them, baskets of red, green and yellow fruit and vegetables were being busily bought and sold. Two more turnings and the map led me to a tall building where many windows blankly watched my approach.

I had found it. Above the impressive double doors, the name glinted imposingly in golden letters—Northern Chronicle. One of the doors was open and I paused, taking stock. Giving a last touch to my hair and moustache I strode inside as purposefully as I could muster. There was a high wooden desk in the hallway in front of me— an ornate ceiling soared overhead and a stern, dark portrait of the Queen almost filled one wall. As I stood there taking it all in a door opened, and a small belligerent man almost fell out, whilst shouting at whoever was inside,

"You don't feckin' print that y' proddy bastard!"

He was dressed in working clothes, blackened by whatever his trade was, and he carried a tall, squashed looking hat which he pushed violently onto his black curls and stamped past me, the smell of burning about him, as he spat, "Get out while y' can son – these are all liars here – black liars!"

A chuckle came from the doorway and a young man in a waistcoat, shirtsleeves and a bright yellow cravat leaned against the frame and looked me up and down. "Bloody Irish! He laughed, "you're not one, are you?"

"No", I replied.

"Well sit," he said, waving in dismissal, then turned and went back through the door behind him.

So, I sat on the bench and waited. People busied themselves and sounds came from deeper within the building but no one seemed to notice me. I turned the brim of my hat through my fingers and stared at Queen Victoria until she became a sinister blob. Then I took a turn at staring at my feet. After a while, a bold cat wandered in and paused to examine me before sauntering to the desk and disappearing around it. This was followed by a voice saying, 'Make sure you get it right!' Stunned for a moment, I did not reply— then it spoke again, 'I told you to make sure you get it right'. By then I was convinced that the cat was advising me in some obscure way, and that I should ignore it for my sanity. "Cats can't speak," I muttered– fixing my gaze firmly on my shoes.

"Of course, they can't!" came back, and standing in front of me holding the smug looking beast in her arms, was a young woman. She wore a smart checked dress and had light brown hair, tidied up in a way mother would approve of, and her smile lit up the hallway. I struggled to my feet and began to apologise, but she swept it away and introduced herself as Maud Lemon, and the cat as Caligula. She couldn't know of course that she was the first woman I had spoken to without a chaperone of any sort, and I found my voice cracking as I began to tell her who I was.

"Yes! Thadeus Vail–I know who you are! You're here for the job as reporter."

She spoke again more seriously, putting Caligula down on the tiles.

"Mr Creed will call you in soon and ask you to write a

sample article—that's what you have to get right or you will be on a train back home again. By the way–I am working on the reception desk here today—you could have spoken to me you know!" I was about to apologise, when the door near us opened again and the same fellow put his head around it and snapped, "You! In here! Maud back to work!"

I jumped up, stumbling over Caligula, and just managed to steady myself as Maud stomped back behind the high desk and left me to it. Inside the room the high window made it seem quite dark. Three people were there, one was at the biggest desk under the window, and two others were standing appraising my entry. A young man who had adopted the effete look of short hair and smooth face nodded, and beside him the one with the yellow cravat and a moustache almost as fine as my own, shook his head as he watched me, my slight limp exaggerated by my trip over Caligula. Behind the desk, an older grey bearded man looked up from something he was writing and cleared his throat,

"Good morning, Thaddeus Vail. These two are Henry Roberts and Nathaniel Parkes–and I am John Creed. I believe you have a letter from me and a map?"

To my horror my mind went blank. This job was what I wanted more than anything– to become a reporter— to write—and I had lost all words.

Creed spoke again slowly as if attempting to communicate with a foreign person, "You do want to take this job, Mr Vail?"

Thoughts of my twin who had never lived one second of his perfect life, and Will going off in his red uniform full of excitement, to end with nothing, churned through my mind and suddenly undid my paralysis. "Yes, Mr Creed, I want it more than anything!"

Both Henry and Nathanial sniggered at this, but Mr Creed silenced them with a look, and they sloped back to their desks and sat down. The last and smallest one of these seemed to be mine. We then commenced our morning briefing. The other two were given reporting assignments to get information about a murder. The weapon, a gun, was still missing—causing consternation to the residents of the town. They left on their mission and I waited for my instructions.

Mr Creed then presented me with a piece of coal.

"I want you to write me an article about this. I will leave you to it. There are books and back copies of the paper over there to help. Make it interesting – and keep it short."

Then he left.

Time seemed to leave the room with him. At first, I just drifted off, staring at the small black rock and dredging up what I already knew about it. Not very much. It burned. It mostly came from the north of the country. It helped make steam to get engines working. It kept us warm. It came from the dark and the ruins of ancient trees. I got lots of dry facts and a few sad and scandalous stories from the books and old newspapers, then I sat down to write. The tenth piece of paper was the one I was finally satisfied with, and I sighed with relief as I blotted it and stretched my inky fingers.

There was no one about then so I went out to ask Maud where I should go next. To my surprise it was already four on the loud clock. Maud told me that Mr Creed had been delayed and she had been told to take me on a tour of the building. She showed me where the type was set up and the huge steam press waited to be powered on for the evening edition of the paper. Several young print room lads were working to unleash it and Iris seemed to know them all. Later we found ourselves back in the corridor with the Queen and Caligula and Mr Creed, who must have returned, coming out of the office. He seemed distracted as if he could not place me for a moment, then handed me a folded note.

"Your piece was very good for a first attempt, but I must supervise the print run now so you may go today and I will see you back here prompt tomorrow. This is where you are staying – I'm sure Maud can point you in the right direction. Good day!" and he rushed back into the office and closed the door briskly behind him.

Maud looked at me and laughed, "Well, get your bag and hat then!"

We walked down the steps and out into the smoky street. The late afternoon was busy and we dodged through the throng as she explained the best way to get to my lodgings. I was very hungry by then so we went into a busy pie shop on the edge of the market I had passed earlier. I bought two and ate one straightaway, carrying the other for later. Afterwards she explained that there were short cuts through the alley ways which went behind the High Street and after checking the address and map with me she said I should be fine at this time of day, but to keep my money close and stay to the centre of the street.

"There is fear about because the murder weapon has not been found, and no one arrested. Steer clear of any Irish – they are angry!" she stated in a matter of fact way as we reached the main High Street where we were to part.

"But how will I know them?"

"Oh, you will – they wear bigger hats and rough cloth-ing," she replied, which seemed a very general description to me. Then pointing out my way, she turned and left me, map and address in my hand, and I watched her weave through the crowd.

Chapter 3

The nearest alley looked dark and I plunged hurriedly into its arched entrance. As I emerged from it into a slightly lighter open yard the strong smell of leather-working overcame me. Hot urine mixed with dead animal flesh and the damp of cured hides added to the manure underfoot, both human and animal. Children played happily in this and women shouted to each other from the windows of what must have been dwellings set all around the yard. There was a well where the alley opened out in the middle and a man and woman argued loudly beside it. To my horror, I realised that he had a high squashed hat very like the man in the Chronicle office, and her clothing was grey and ragged. I looked down and headed past them with purpose, but they took no notice of me and having gained a little distance, I slowed down. That was a mistake!

My arm was grabbed and twisted up behind my back as a salty hand pressed into my mouth and I seemed to fly sideways into another dark opening. A low voice hissed into my ear, "Shut the fuck up – no sound and I'll let you go!" I nodded and the disgusting hand released my mouth. I saw his face clearly for a moment but was pushed against moss covered bricks, his other arm across my wind-pipe.

"Take this and keep it safe until I come for it. I know who you are and where you're living. Very bad things will happen if you tell anyone – and that girl you were with – we've got her now and it will be even worse for her if you let me down. It's a signal for a big event– you will be told where to take it when the time is right. Tell no one!" and with that I was shoved out into the alley again holding a cloth sack and gasping for air.

People passing looked at me without interest and it was only when I reached the open street and rested on a wall, shaking, that I looked into the bag and caught the metallic glint and shape of a gun. My valise was still safe, but the map and address were gone from my other hand. I remember little of reaching my lodgings. A white aproned grocer had come out from behind his counter to give me directions. He knew which house it was from the street name that I remembered from the map.

A tall, newish building sat, guarded by black railings on a wide dirt street. A servant came to the bell pull and looked me up and down appraisingly before leading me to the kitchen where the landlady supervised the clearing of the last meal. Flushed with kitchen heat yet still managing to seem severe, Mrs Furness introduced herself, told me I was too late for supper, explained the rules of the house then sent me up to my room at the very top.

I had to use the narrow servants' stairs which twisted dark and steep up from the kitchen. The room was bare of ornament, a bed along one wall and a press at its head beside a small chest. A sagging armchair sighed in the corner. I lit the one candle and went to look out of the window. Down below, light streamed out from the kitchen onto an empty yard. Beyond that it was hard to see anything and no sound carried. The heat from the kitchen must have risen from two floors below as it was quite warm. Unwrapping the second pie, I sank down into the chair and stretched out. The pastry had hardened a little and the contents were some sort of meat. I began to feel a little calmer and as I ate I pictured Mother and Father at their third or fourth course in the vicarage dining room, in glum emptiness at the absence of all their sons, with Bridie silently bringing in aromatic dishes while Etta sat obediently at one end painfully supressing her sixteen year old energy.

Gathering the pastry crumbs into the paper and dropping it on the chest I opened my travel bag and put the few items it contained away, avoiding even looking at the sack on the floor by the door. I went through the last two days' events in my mind as I did this. The cold dawn ride in the trap from Prickwillow along the river Lark and into Ely to catch the slow stopping train to Peterborough; the exhilaration of travelling alone once Ben the coachman had left me in Ely and the excited feeling of having made my own choice for the first time. I was following my greatest desire and I was not going to let the incident in the yard eat into my dreams. After kicking the gun bag under the bed, I undressed and lay down, realising how tired I really was. My shorter leg, which caused me to limp, ached a little but I had never felt so alive— as if I had broken out of a prison and found the freedom that for so long had only seemed to be for others.

Just for a moment on waking next day, I looked for Bridie opening the heavy velvet curtains and the slatted light falling through the bars of the nursery window. Then I remembered freedom had a price. I would have to make my own way down to the yard where the pump and outhouse were shared with servants and lodgers. My legs worked well despite the ache, and I found myself in the busy kitchen where Mrs Furness directed two young girls with plates of crackling bacon and pink fried eggs back and forth through a swinging door. Before I could speak, she thrust a metal bowl in my hands, snapping,

"Yours for shaving – pump outside," then turned her back on me.

Outside, the paved yard was wet with earlier rain and a queue waited to fill their bowls and hurry back into the house. After a perilous slopping journey back up the stairs I had a quick cold shave then made my way back down to a plate of food. Tea was served in abundance and I was to learn that this was always the case in Linden House. The lodgers were men of all ages, who came and went in a way which seemed to multiply their numbers every day. Next to me that first morning sat a young man about my age. He wore a rough jacket, a grubby checked muffler wrapped around his neck, and a large cloth cap lay on the table beside his plate. His face was round and his hair an orange colour I had not often seen before. He sniffed loudly as his nose ran constantly. I introduced myself and he grunted and nodded, seeming to mumble a name like Jim, and then jumped up and left. The two serving girls clearing the plates put their heads together whispering and giggling as they watched this.

"Haven't your mothers told you it's rude to whisper?" I called out to them and this seemed to increase their mirth even further as they pushed through the swing door and out of sight. I realised then that everyone had gone and my voice had sounded so like my mother's that a shiver went up my spine. As I stepped outside and headed to the Chronicle office, I knew that Will would have followed the girls, and asked for a reprimand from Mrs. Furness for their behaviour. As mother repeatedly commented, he would have taken the bold and manly route in any situation. I had thought to leave him behind, but I supposed he wouldn't leave me.

I had hidden the gun safely in my bag under the bed and I decided I would tell Mr. Creed all about it despite the warnings. The sun broke through a smoky sky and people and traffic moved with purpose. I smiled as I thought, "They are off to work. I am off to work." I forced the ghost of Will behind me with each step.

Reaching the Chronicle office, I found one of the young men from the print room at the desk. On finding that he did not know where Miss Lemon was and was not happy to be relegated to her job, my heart sank. Somewhere, she was being held against her will. The loud clock struck nine while Queen Victoria scowled and I decided I had better wait a while before telling Mr. Creed what had happened the night before. I must not put Maud into further danger. I would give it another day then go to the police.

The others were all there just as the day before and we started our meeting. Henry was to be sent to interview a man who was planning a horse and dog show, which was a big civic event in the town, and Nathaniel to speak to people annoyed by the extra mud surrounding a town fountain. Mr. Creed turned to me then,

"I want you to go up to Durham. There was a sad event in Esh. Two young lads fell down the main shaft of the pit and broke their necks. The readers love a good tragedy – they even buy postcard souvenirs of them!" he chuckled. "So, after your wonderful piece on coal yesterday – I thought you could represent it best. They like lots of detail too – don't spare the graphics!" He leaned over and handed me the coins to pay for the train and the address of the young men's family.

"When you get to Durham just ask for Esh – they'll point you to the right wagonway. Last train back is at half past nine this evening so you should have plenty of time before the press rolls. Good luck!"

As if noting my apprehension, Nathaniel spoke up, "Let me go with Thadeus Mr. Creed —I know the area and the people and can keep him right. We will be back early afternoon so there's still time for me to cover the fountain story."

The editor paused, a little taken aback, then nodded, "Very well – it's probably for the best." With that he turned his back on me and took up a pen.

"As you haven't been to the coalfields before I would suggest that losing that top hat would be a good idea," Nathaniel said in a less friendly manner, indicating that I should leave it on my desk. I couldn't go out bareheaded of course but Henry saved the day producing a large flat cap from a drawer. "I'll put yours away safely – don't worry! The Irish usually keep themselves to themselves but you don't want to annoy them, do you?"

"Irish!" I spluttered.

"Oh yes – there are a lot of Irish there I think."

Taking my hat, he turned and left me to it – a thousand

questions spinning around unanswered in my head. Could the gun man be there? Would I be caught again? Why did no one seem to notice Maud was missing? For a brief moment the safety of Prickwillow seemed almost enticing, then Caligula's commanding cry brought my attention back to the dead mouse he was laying at my feet. He was probably hungry—I supposed Maud would have fed him if she had been there, and I feared the worst.

All the way to the station I managed to walk as steadily as possible— a smart young man with a limp would be easy to spot— even with the flat cap. Nathaniel was not inclined to talk and no one approached me as my mind churned over the image of the gun nestling in my travel bag and the taste of that hand on my mouth. I wondered if the serving girls would go in to clean and search through my belongings for something to gossip about, and I felt an agony of guilt churn my stomach as we paid and went onto the platform. A huge cloud filled the air as the steam engine approached like a dragon from its cave and squealed to a stop in front of us. Negotiating the heavy handle and high steps, we got into a carriage occupied by a well-dressed man and three women in black.

"Don't ask me anything until we get there," Nathaniel said in a low voice when I opened my mouth to try and make conversation.

The station at Durham was just like Darlington, busy with people rushing here and there, and we changed to a smaller train for Esh. This one was all wood, hard shiny seats, some open carriages and lots of chatter from children, women and some working men. It moved onto a branch line and swayed much more noticeably as the landscape outside changed from green fields and hills to giant dark wheels out-lined against the sky, and tall brick beehive shapes, chimneys belching smoke around them. The smell of sulphur floated through the windows of the carriage and a sort of dust hung in the air above the perfect straight rows of dwellings which lay amongst the industry. A few people got off at Esh and hurried away, leaving me and Nathaniel alone on the platform above the tightly packed town.

He indicated my satchel, "You do have a notebook and pen in there don't you—not just a hairbrush, handkerchief and spare Macassar oil?" I opened it to show him but he just waved it away without looking in, "When we get to the Kelly's house, act respectful but don't scrimp on finding any gruesome details. It's down the third street along. There's something I must do but I'll be back in time for the next train. I'm relying on you, Thadeus."

"But which house do I—?" I began, but before I could ask another word, he rushed off down one of the streets and left me to it.

It turned out the Kelly family was easy to find, as the first passer-by I asked was eager to show me the way, with much sighing about the great sadness of it all. Identical streets stretched out down a hillside, but the Kelly's house stood out, with black curtains at the small front window and chairs set out by the door occupied by three women—black crows in a row. One of them held what looked like a necklace in her fingers and they all chanted words together as she slipped the beads around. As a vicar's son, I recognised that they were praying and took off my large cap to show respect. They took no notice of me and eventually a tall man in a long robe bent his head to exit the house and placed himself between the women and me.

"They're ready now, ladies," he interrupted them in a voice used to being listened to, "Go in." Then to me he said in an offhand way, "Who are you? What do you want?"

His bright blue gaze observed me coldly and I found my face almost touching his chest, as he was considerably taller.

"I'm from the Northern Chronicle," I stuttered and stepped back as he replied,

"Father. It's Father Lodge"

For a moment I was back in the nursery attempting to explain some failed algebra task – desperate not to be beaten for my stupidity.

"I'm from the Northern Chronicle, *Father Lodge*," he repeated slowly emphasising the final word, "That is my term of address young man," he continued, "the family are expecting you I believe – please show some courtesy."

Then he turned and swished off up the long street without looking back. Still nervous, I stepped through the open door and found myself at the foot of two open lidded coffins each containing the shrouded corpses of boys. Their faces were the only part of them visible and their heads wrapped in cloth could not disguise the swelling and bruising. One of the women pushed back her shawl and spoke,

"These are my youngest – John Joseph and Patrick." She touched each one as she spoke his name. "One year apart – John Joseph is fifteen and Patrick fourteen. They are drivers and proud of it – they love those ponies. Half-marrows they are by now – sharing their earnings – been trappers before that."

I could see she was younger than I'd thought when she removed her shawl. Her hair was still dark and pulled up on her head – skin smooth and sad eyes clear.

"You'll write about them then?" she asked and I realised that I had not taken out my notebook or pencil and was just staring in shock at the sight before me. My voice cracked as I spoke, "Yes – that is why I am here. Can you tell me everything?"

She spoke quietly in another language to the other two women and indicated that I follow her to the back room. This held a blackened range with a high mantel above it and a table covered in a sort of dark green plush cloth. Religious statues and pictures mixed with those of dogs and a black framed photograph of stiffly serious people. In one corner, an open wooden stair went up to a hole in the ceiling and opposite, a wooden press took up the rest of the wall. Through the back window I could see the bricks of the yard wall. We both sat down and she began her story.

The boys were the youngest of nine – four daughters still lived at home with her and the older three were married and gone, her husband dead of fever five years before. They had been at work all night and got into the cage to return to bank but it was accidentally drawn right up to the pulley wheels and tipped. John Joseph had tried to hang on and stop his brother from falling but lost his own grip. They both tumbled out, hitting heads off the sides on the way and landing broken at the bottom of the deep shaft, bones snapped and heads burst. All the while she spoke, she stared out of the window until finally she turned and looked at me,

"We've no man at the pit now. They'll want the house back soon."

Just then a voice interrupted us from the other room and she rose, shaking off the story and straightening her shoulders, "We'll manage though I suppose—I have my daughters' husbands to help and a little money from the mine for my loss. I must attend to my sons now – so good day."

I passed the coffins without looking, a sweetish smell following me as I headed quickly back up the street to the station. A train was waiting, catching its steamy breath, but there was no sign of Nathaniel anywhere and I wondered what friends he could have in that place that were more important than his job. Wanting to get away as soon as I could and erase those swollen faces from my mind, I made the choice to jump on and find my own way back.

Two elderly women were talking loudly opposite me in the way of the hard of hearing, and I realised they were chatting about not going back to Durham until the following week. They tutted at my rude interruption to their conversation but confirmed that I should get off at the next stop and wait for a train back in the right direction.

So, for the first time, I found myself in Cornsay Colliery.

Chapter 4

The platform emptied quickly and I sat on a wooden bench to wait for the next train up the line. Taking out my notebook I began to make a start on the article I would write. I was deciding between, 'Horrible death in the mine' and 'A mother bereft' for a title, when a loud wail filled the air.

The cinder path in front of the station began to fill up with a river of men, boots clattering and crunching as it flowed both ways. In one direction there were clean faces, tidy shirts, hats and mufflers as they trudged along talking, laughing and calling out greetings to the dust black group in the other direction, steps heavy after eight hours of work. There was nowhere to conceal myself on the open platform so I just sat and took in the transformation of the quiet place. As the downward men reached their own streets, they peeled off the main flow, and suddenly he was there – the man who had forced the gun upon me. For a second he looked straight at me and nodded a greeting, then he ducked behind the up-stream flow of men and vanished completely.

In a few minutes, both groups had passed, my assailant with them, and the platform seemed vast, empty and exposed. My heart pounded and my stomach sank. My head spun with questions. Had he followed me? How did he know where I was that day? I had to get away, to hide myself but I also wanted to find him – pin him down and get some answers. Without taking stock of what I was doing I found myself heading down one of the streets, each house watching me with one dark windowed eye. The rumbling rattle of a horse and cart and the sight of a small child running out in front of it happened at the same moment. The child wore a long dirty greyish garment and was laughing gleefully, unaware of any danger. In a second I had somehow managed to grab an edge of the cloth and yanked hard, pulling the child on top of me and throwing us both back onto the ground. The cart slowed but carried on, its driver shouting, "Take care of yer' bairn – idiot!"

For a moment I was paralysed, unable to catch my breath, deafened by the open mouthed wailing of the wriggling bundle on top of me. Somehow it was raised up into the air and I rolled over, gasping, and found myself facing a pair of scuffed shoes and the hem of a dress. An angry voice shouted above me,

"You are a wee monster – inside with you now!"

The feet and wailing disappeared, followed by the sound of a door slamming. I rolled over and got up slowly, retrieving my notebook and cap from the dusty ground and glanced around for the gun giver— just in case— when the door opened again and a young woman stepped out. Her open smiling face was topped by pale auburn hair escaping from its restraint like eels from a bucket, her figure slim and neat in its plain dress.

"Thank you, sir – Mammy says 'thank you' too. He's a little handful is Kieran – Da says it's his red hair — just to tease me — as its mine too. I'm Ina — Ina Maguire. Who are you? Not a collier — that I can see!"

Something in me really wanted to impress her, but the words that came out of my mouth in Mother's voice made me cringe, "You and your family should take more care if the child is so wilful. How could he escape like that?"

To my surprise she just laughed, "Come away in and take a tea and a sit down — it seems your nerves must be shot to forget your own name." She took my hand and pulled me in.

"I do apologise. I am Thadeus Vail – newspaper reporter for the Northern Chronicle. I got separated from my colleague, then got lost and took the wrong train at Esh."

Inside it was dark but so like the Kelly's cottage that I almost looked for the coffins. The back room had the same table, press and black range and the window showing the bricks of the yard. Kieran sat in a wooden chair which seemed to restrain him and was banging on the table with a spoon. There was no sign of anyone else. Ina made tea at the range and we sat on two of the nine chairs to drink it.

"So," she started "are you at Esh for the two poor Kelly lads, or are you on the hunt for Fenians?"

I let the hot sweet tea cool while I composed my answer. "Yes — the Kellys — that's where I was – talking to their poor mother. It was a chilling sight those boys in boxes."

She laughed again in reply, "Death is life here you know! The mines eat people up so you can be warm in winter and catch your trains!" Breaking off, she picked up the baby and carried him to a crib in the front room by the wall. I finished my tea and was just about to get up and leave when the ladder began to creak and a black shape pushed through the hole in the ceiling and descended. It was a woman, very like Ina but stouter and more careworn.

"Who the devil is this, Ina?" she called over my head.

"Shush Ma – I'm settling Kieran," came back in a loud whisper – so I introduced myself again. Her presence was almost as intimidating as Mother's and the old feelings of inadequacy came back again, tightening my throat and taking hold of my voice. Ina saved me by coming back into the room. At first, she said something in the same language Mrs. Kelly had used to her relatives, and this seemed to soften her.

"So, to thank him for his bravery I will take Mr. Vail back to the station and make sure he gets that train for Durham," Ina spoke slowly and clearly, sharing a knowing look with her mother.

"We all thank you for saving little Kieran – he has such a desire to get close to horses and all beasts. One of my sons must have left the door ajar after himself when he went off to the back shift. It is all such a rush with one lot coming in and another out."

She spoke directly to me for the first time. Ina had picked up a shawl and indicated that we would go out the back together. Thanking Mrs. Maguire for the tea I was surprised to see her jump at the sound of her name, as if it was a secret I should not know. Outside in the alley, sheets and clothing flapped and waved at us and women passed, nodding or calling out to Ina, sometimes in that language that seemed to flow from a memory that I couldn't quite reach. I floated in a kind of dream, watching her walk ahead of me all sunlight smiles and friendly chatter through the dusty sulphur smell of the air.

"You asked me about finding Fenians," I said to her shape which was vanishing behind a flapping sheet, "What does that mean?" Mr. Creed had spoken of the murder the other day and the fact that there seemed to be a Fenian connection.

She stopped dead and pulled me round the washing line.

"Not here — come with me for a walk down to the field past the brick kilns. There's few about there —we can talk."

We turned and headed back down towards the brick beehive shapes in the distance.   "What are they for?" I panted, trying to keep up with her.

"For a reporter you don't know much!" she laughed, "they're coke ovens. They cook the coal to make it. Gets rid of gasses and makes good fuel for factories to use – that's what my brother Thomas said anyway. Those further along make bricks for building with."

We were passing them by then and the smell was even stronger. Not far beyond we came to a fence which bordered a green field, past the busy wagonway that ran beside the kilns. Ina climbed the fence and I followed, trying to make it look as easy as she did. I had no desire to look even more of a weakling in her eyes than I felt I already did. We sank down on a hillock with our backs to the ovens and the town.

"Tell me about you and your family," I asked. She sighed and began,

"So, my Da and Mammy they came from Ireland. It was a long while ago and a hard journey they had to get here.

There was a great hunger and many people died – but there was food and work over here in England – as we are all the same country of course – so they came. We were all born here, my sisters and brothers too. They don't talk much of their journeys, but many people do, and they want Ireland to be free to rule itself." She stopped to watch a magpie land nearby then take off when I moved my foot.

"So, is that it? Are all Irish Fenians then, because of that?"

She looked up. "No – of course not! And I couldn't be telling you who is as you are a newspaper reporter of course! Some would like a proper war to get revenge for what the government did in Ireland in those days and to free the country. The government in England took our crops, our cattle, and our grain and sold it on to other countries too. There was nothing left to eat when the potato crop failed. Most people lived on them before that. Can you imagine that—nothing to eat at all? So, we died or left. Many came here or went to America. I have uncles there Da says, but they cannot write and they don't know where we live anyway."

My stomach sank as I remembered that I had that gun in my lodgings as a signal for something. Could people here be part of the murder in Darlington or planning something even worse?

As she spoke, the freckles on her pale skin danced and the blue of her eyes sparkled like the Lark River in summer. Hoping that she had been misinformed by her family and only needed to hear both sides of the story of Ireland, I decided to try and put her right.

"Ina, everyone knows that there is much drunkenness,

violence and laziness among the Irish. Many believe it was their own primitive ways that led to that hunger — they could have found work to save themselves — the government even set up building schemes for them."

For a few moments she was silent, then she began to laugh,

"Oh dear! If everyone knows, then it must be true, cara! Me Da and brothers take their drunken laziness down the mine and risk death every day so you can have your steam engines, your factories, your warm hearth in winter and even your newspaper presses." She finished with an amused shake of the head. Leaning forward she picked at the dusty grass and found a piece long enough to place between her thumbs and blow a whistled note. Then she changed the subject in a final way.

"Do you believe in fairies?" she asked without looking up.

"I've never thought of them," I replied cautiously, not really understanding where our conversation had gone.

"The fairies are from the ancient Tuatha race – once angels in heaven, they were cast out as a punishment for their pride. They live in palaces under the sea and in lakes but mainly in caves underneath the hills. Their name became Sidhe, the name for earthen mounds, because the earth was where they lived. They have all the riches of the earth but they can do nothing with it for themselves. Perhaps the mines are like that – my people, like the fairies!" She turned then, and leaning in she kissed me. The shape of her body was warm against me and my hands shook when I eventually pulled away, heart thumping. Her smile lingered. "Never be tempted by a fairy kiss – the madness of love will fall upon you!"

Then, as if nothing had happened at all, she commented briskly,

"Well that's the beginning of our story then! Don't write of Fenians in your newspaper – or tell anyone about them or they may come and get you! Come on or you'll miss the next train too and I have sewing work to collect." As we walked back up over the wagonway, past the brick kilns and the alley towards the station, I imagined taking her hand and pulling her towards me again and silently cursed both fairies and Fenians.

She watched me board the train, then pulled her shawl up over her head and called above the churning hiss of steam, "Find a reason to come back soon –I would like that!" Then she turned and walked briskly away without looking back.

Chapter 5

It was a short journey back to Durham, though my thoughts skittered between anxiety over the possible presence of the gun man on the train and the feelings that Ina had stirred in my mind and body. Once I stood safely again on the main platform at Durham my heart slowed down.

I found the Darlington train without a problem and climbed into a carriage of eight. The landscape rolling past the window, a patchwork of green fields and industry, covered a bed of history. Forests and farms slept beneath it, woken by pit sinkers and the scrabble for earth's treasures far below. Ina's fairies would not have had a chance to save anything, but up above plenty gained wealth from them. Of course, coal fired the changes which built the factories and sank the mines, fuelling steam driven dreams – engines to drain the fen where I grew up, to pull the trains and power the presses so newspapers and books could be easily printed and sold. Machinery of every sort puffed away on the power of coal.

I saw myself fancifully putting all of this into my article and Mr. Creed congratulating me with chief reporter status after reading it. This image brought to mind the reasons why I so wanted to succeed at the job. Long years trapped at home, never travelling or making friends, not allowed any independent pursuits in case I took ill or strained myself – even coming to wish that I was somehow a changeling and my true parents were on their way to claim me for a life of excitement and danger.

Father, in his clergyman's pomposity, read mainly the Bible and the Book of Prayer and his morning paper – Mother not even that. Anything Will brought home from school helped to open a crack of light in my mind, but the main material available was that newspaper. I read every word, every story, every advertisement, perused every drawing as if my life depended on it. After Will had gone for good – into the Royal Artillery to our parents' disgust – not to clerical college to join the church – I could picture the places he had gone from my reading. Africa was so far away and the battle of Amoaful even more distant. They fought tribesmen in order to keep the place civilised and the rightful property of our Empress.

The letter said he was shot in the leg, but saved. He himself wrote to say he would soon be home and tell us of his heroic deeds in person. The last letter, only three weeks later, told us of his death. He had developed a disease brought on by his wound and was buried there in the hot soil of Africa. No medal was given for his efforts but to our parents he became a saint. From that time, the big idea began to take shape. If Will could be a dead hero then I could become a newspaper reporter and escape when I reached twenty one, taking my life and death into my own hands.

Those feelings of the day I saw the advertisement in Father's paper for the job of reporter on Northern Chronicle rolled back to me, as the train puffed into a siding waiting for the signal to move on. I knew then that I was leaving. I, who had rarely even been into Ely on my own, was going. The editor offered me the job by return of post. When Mother's cajoling, admonishing, scolding and outright shouting had finished I said farewell to Etta and shook hands with Father, Mother turning her back and refusing to speak further, hugged Bridie, then climbed into the chaise with Ben and left Prickwillow to start living.

The flow of those memories carried me through the bustle and smoke of the station at Darlington. The weather was slightly warmer as I walked back to the Chronicle offices and I munched another pie bought along the way. Henry and Mr. Creed were busily writing up copy for the day and everywhere was activity as we prepared for print. Nathaniel punctured this bubble of activity with his loud entrance, carrying a tray of buns and tea for everyone.   "Where on earth did you get to, Thadeus? I looked all over for you —surely you know not to wander off in a strange place! Mummy must have taught you that!"

"But—I didn't—it wasn't—,"I gasped.

"Well, I've been back and interviewed the man about the statue since. Enjoy your bun!"

Angry that he was lying but also strangely in defence of Mother's reputation, I settled at my desk and dipped a pen in the inkwell – then my mind went blank. A scrunched up piece of paper hit my head and Nathaniel sniped, "Oh dear – Thadeus was late and has no ideas either Mr. Creed. Tut tut!"

Creed glanced up briefly, "Get on with it Vail – and no

dawdling next time – I can't afford to pay someone who cannot write!"

"I'm sorry Mr. Creed – I got lost."

"Getting lost is not good enough," he muttered without raising his head again and Nathaniel smirked knowingly in the background. Somehow that inspired me– blood and guts is what people wanted so that is what they would get – and my pen was flying across the paper. Nathaniel made sure I could not speak to him alone and discover what he had been doing in Esh Winning, and it was only after the thrill of seeing my first article sent to print that I remembered I had still not seen Maud and there was a gun in my room.

It was later that day when I left and made my way up the muddy hill to the high street. Determined not to be accosted again I walked a longer way around, avoiding the crowded yards. There was some food left for me on the table in the lodging house and I ate it alone afraid to go back up those narrow stairs. When I finally reached the top of them, I breathed deeply and pushed the door hard – banging it back against the cupboard. My candle showed no one was there and I shut it more softly and began to undress. In bed, I felt for my bag and the gun. It was still there. Blowing out the candle I decided I really must tell someone about it the next day and drifted into a fitful sleep where Ina and Maud were laid out in boxes and Mrs. Kelly and the man with the gun danced a jig around them.

The next day rain made rivers down the window-pane and my good leg ached. I dressed slowly and moved the gun to another hiding place –the inner pocket of my spare waistcoat hanging in the press. The yard was cold and unpleasant and I decided to find a barber to shave me in the comfort of his shop. Mrs. Furness said a polite good morning as I passed through the kitchen, while the servant girls threw suspicious glances to each other behind her back. Trying to quell my fears that they had found the gun while cleaning, I ate a swift breakfast and set off the way I had come the previous evening. Even with all that had happened so far, I still felt the thrill of knowing I was going to my workplace – to the life I wanted.

My assignment was to report on a water fountain being moved from the street it was flooding and taken to some parkland just outside the town. Workmen, some looking suspiciously Irish, were removing pieces of it onto a cart for transport, their feet and legs soaked by the mud infested puddles it stood in, and their outerwear by the heavy rain. The fountain had been generously donated to the townsfolk by the Temperance Society a few years before and some were present. They busied themselves handing out printed sheets on the evils of drink and the wonderful gift of God's pure water from the sky sent to nourish us. Several passers-by called out to them regarding the warming properties of brandy as opposed to freezing sticky mud, and two of the workmen ostentatiously shared a stone jug of beer before continuing with their task.

Groups of onlookers melted away to watch a dancing bear on a chain across the street. Its owner prodded it with a stick to help it dance, and it made an entertaining roaring noise which added excitement and a little fear to the spectacle. I took copies of the printed speech from the temperance men and spoke to them and the beer drinkers before wandering across to watch the bear. After a few more minutes its owner pulled on the chain shouting a command and it fell to the ground panting, while he collected coins in a hat. Feeling happy with my day so far, I limped away, ignoring a child's loud comment,

"Look there—he walks like a bear too!"

There was no Bridie to shout back or confront the child's parents, stemming the laughter that we knew would follow, so I just slowed down and walked through the pain to the first barber's I came across. The shop was quite dark inside but there was only a short wait before I climbed into the leather chair and sank back in comfort. There was some chatter amongst the customers but the man working on me did not indulge in the empty questions that the barber I had been taken to in Ely enjoyed. I could drift as he lathered my face and took care to trim my prized moustache, until it dawned on me that all the talk was of the murder – the Irish and the gun. One man believed that all the Irish should be searched and locked up until the gun was found. Another stated that it was well known that they had more guns anyway, and explosives.

"They steal from the rail works you know and the mines. They don't have the same morals as us – it's because they're foreign really!" he said, speaking in a way that he felt no one could disagree with.

The barber working on me spoke quietly, "Their country is part of this one too. We run it." The lilt in his voice reminded me of Mrs. Kelly. The first man opined that he probably had a point and that maybe not all Irish were Fenian bastards, then moved on to talk of the current show at one of the music halls. Without any sort of slip the barber finished my shave and betrayed no feeling as he invited the man to step up next. The rest had eased my limp and stepping out into the rain, I knew a little of how he must have felt.

I bought a bag of fish scraps in the market and gave them to Caligula who was waiting on the steps of the Chronicle as if he'd known that's what I would do. The print lad, taking his turn on the desk, wouldn't let him in because he was wet. Still no Maud. Only Nathaniel was in the office and he seemed to have become friendlier, even offering me a tea to drink as I wrote. He put it on my desk with a smile and told me he was writing about a fight the previous night in town where two Irishmen outside a music hall were scrapping over a woman. He had interviewed the woman who had given him all the details. His mood however changed instantly when I asked him about Esh.

"Irish eh? I sympathised, "But where did you get to the other day—who were you meeting?"

"Thadeus—you're a baby in all of this! I had to meet an old friend—it was private, do you understand?" he snapped and refused to be drawn further.

After that, we both set to work and this time my writing flowed, partly because I had the printed sheets from the teetotallers and partly because I now believed I could do it. Henry and Mr. Creed came in soon after and set to their writing as Nathaniel leaned back stretched and sighed, "Well that's me done. I'm off upstairs with it." He stood and swept past my desk knocking the rest of my tea all over the paper. The lines swam out of shape joining into an inky sea. "Oh dear – you are clumsy, Thadeus, perhaps it's because your balance isn't the best, eh?" he sneered.

Mr. Creed tutted and dug his watch out of his waistcoat pocket, "That gives you twenty minutes to get it done Mr. Vail– then I want you out again. A cart has overturned in the market and there may be injuries. Hurry please. I will not tolerate this shoddiness!"

As I struggled to clear the mess up it had become clear to me that Nathaniel was not to be trusted. Outside, after cobbling another shorter article together, the sky still loured although the rain had stopped.

Over in the market there was chaos as people shouted amid the commotion, pushing and shoving to grab fruit from the cart and any that was slipping around in the mud. A small group surrounded a prone figure. A horse was being held by a boy nearby and the cart was still upended behind it. Crunching and slipping across the slime of apples and pears, I approached them and tried to assess the scene. A man whose long coat swished wetly around his ankles, bowler hat shining with rain answered my query of, 'what happened here?' with a sigh.

"He's dead. Horse alright. Goods ruined."

A sobbing woman knelt beside the carter and three others surrounded him. One of them looked up from under her shawl,

"He's Tom Clark if you want to know. He fell onto the horse and frightened it and it bolted – cart skid in the mud. He was ill, but had to work. No more though. No more." She trailed off and put her arm around the sobbing woman.

It was the first time I had seen a freshly dead corpse. No coins on the eyelids, arrangement of the arms, face polished and arranged in a peaceful expression. Tom Clark's face was contorted in a painful grimace and his eyes opened to the grey sky – arms stretched out, curling fingers grasping a last hold on life.

"Five little ones to keep too." The first man said behind me. They had cleared another cart by then and four market traders pulled his body from the sticky mud and placed it there. One woman threw her shawl over it and a dark procession was about to set off, when it was halted by a newly arrived police officer with a raised hand. He walked around the horse, ignoring the now wailing women, and removed the shawl with a dramatic flourish.

"Name and circumstances?" he snapped at the group. The bowler-hatted man stepped forward and supplied all the details, which helped me significantly until my scribbles were interrupted by the officer's direct question,

"And who might you be?"

My voice shook a little as I replied,

"I am a reporter – for the Northern Chronicle. I'm new here. Mr. Creed sent me." At Creed's name he seemed to soften and even smiled a little,

"Send Mr. Creed my best wishes, lad. I am Constable I 'Anson by the way – make sure you spell it right." Then he turned and ushered the mourning group off with a cheery, "Straight to the mortuary with him then – don't want him getting all bloated, do we?"

The market let them go and moved on with its day. I hung on, wondering whether to buy a pie, when I saw a familiar figure outlined in the doorway of the inn on the corner. The man with the gun was looking straight at me – same big hat and long black jacket. Nodding, he lifted it slightly and then turned and sauntered off. Without a thought I set off after him. I wanted to know who he was, where Maud was and how long did I have to keep the gun for.   My heart pounding, I reached the corner he had just taken and saw him vanishing into a dark brick archway. Almost slipping over on the muddy ground I turned into another yard, a version of the one off the High Street.

Rain bounced off the puddles on the cobbles, clothes flapped wetly from lines overhead. People called to each other from window to window and children leaned in doorways to shelter from the rain. There was no sign of him and the children I asked seemed not to understand me. I had to give up then and had turned back, angry and frustrated at my situation when a woman's voice called from above,

"Careful love – he's not what you think he is!"

Surprised, I looked all around but no face showed at any window. Heading back to the Chronicle building one thought did come to me – Constable I'Anson had sounded just like Mrs. Kelly and the Maguires. He was Irish too.

Chapter 6

My article on the demise of Tom Clark was suitably gory with no details missed and Mr. Creed allowed it on the first news page after the advertisements. There was a thrill to getting my own copy even though my name was not on it. Nathaniel's was right beside it headed 'More Irish troubles!'

A few more days rolled by and I had even got used to moving the gun to a different hiding place every morning and the fact that no one seemed troubled that Maud was missing.

After the paper was put to bed one day, Henry suggested that I might go with him to visit a music hall. For a moment I imagined Mother and Father's reaction to such a suggestion. To them, music halls were an attraction for rabble drawn together by the lure of low theatre. In fact, such places were calculated to promote evil in all its forms. They dressed this up somewhat as a Christian concern for the poor. How worrying it was to think they would spend what little they had on music hall and be driven to pawn or sell their clothing and eventually resort to stealing just to stay alive. However, my parents' concern was tempered by the desire not to have to pay heavier poor rates themselves to support those newly made paupers.

There had been no music hall in Prickwillow of course

and Mother and Father could not supply me with information as to what was so attractive to these poor people that they would keep going back to their ruin. Their attitude was enough to drive me to sample its delights for myself of course, so after a meal in the chop house on the corner of the market Henry and I set off together for the Theatre Tent, a few streets past the market and thankfully not down any yards.

Knots of people joined us as we headed towards the inn which fronted the field where the tent was set up. The air crackled with excitement and there was much laughter and friendly jostling. A child in a green and red costume was handing out sheets to the gathering crowd which proclaimed with a flourish, 'Mr. Allen's Excelsior Amphitheatre and Temple of Varieties' above the drawing of a beautiful young woman on a fine horse. Several people were drinking from stoppered clay bottles and Henry bought us one each from a busy stall set up outside the inn. The beer was strong and soon numbed thoughts of Maud and Ina and the Fenians, although it took more than one refill to lose my anxieties about the rougher element and obvious groups of Irish that surrounded us. A bell rang loudly and the crowd surged forward to the entrance to the passage at the side of the inn.

People were funnelled through and out to a tree hung path, which led past a tall stone wall on one side and stables and sheds on the other. This brought us to a table being manned by two muscled men wearing only striped trousers and boots who took our entrance fee before we passed through to the field behind. A huge tent flapped at its centre with horses grazing behind it and music rose from somewhere beyond the noise of the crowd.

Henry and I pushed through to the entrance and managed to find places on a bench not far from the stage area, where we enjoyed our third beer and waited expectantly. He stretched and leaned back surprising me by asking, "Nathaniel doesn't like you – does he?"

I laughed ruefully, "Jealous, I suppose!"

"Well, he was the bright light before you came! He's good you know. A good reporter. Doesn't want Mr. Creed taking to you – and doesn't want Maud taking to you either."

Stunned, I almost choked on the last dregs from the jar, "Maud – where is she? Where is Maud?" I stood up to let a couple past.

"I'm not sure – she's usually....."Henry began but a loud trumpet blast drowned out the rest of his reply and the show began.

All the gas lights around us were turned down, leaving only a couple illuminating the stage as a woman walked on and bowed. She was dressed in quite an ordinary way and about Mother's age but the crowd seemed to love her as wild clapping and cheers broke out. She silenced them with a wave and began a song which seemed to be about somebody's bloomers. There was a rousing chorus which ended with,

'So, she left them hanging out the back!' to which we all joined in with gusto. Her character and performance captured me and I found myself shouting, 'Come back Janet!' with the rest of the audience when she left the stage. After a few moments, a horse was ridden up into the lights. The young woman from the flyer was seated on it and two others held the reins and pirouetted around. I had never seen women in such revealing clothing and was mesmerised by their shape and the way the sparkling crystals on their costumes caught the light when they moved.

For some reason the crowd had grown quiet and the girl spoke three words, "For my mother," before standing up in the saddle and balancing on one leg. Then music started and all three dazzled with acrobatic feats while the horse walked around the small space. The cheers were deafening at the end and Henry leaned over and hissed in my ear, "That's Rose Allen. Her mother died just a few months ago – she was remarkable, everyone misses her – Rose is only fifteen you know!"

The magic had captured me by then and I felt real sadness for someone I knew nothing of. Colour, excitement and laughter followed on with a singer called Mr. Hales who told jokes; someone who seemed to swallow the blade of a sword; and a voluptuous woman who represented a naked Greek statue to cat calls and descriptions of what they would like to do to her from the drunkest audience members. I managed to control myself but she did appear in my dreams for a while afterwards.

The final act was shocking in a different way. He wore a tail-coat and a colourful top hat and was accompanied by one of the girls from the horse riding act. He introduced himself as 'The Great Maskelyne' and did a few conjuring tricks before snapping his fingers in the air which brought on two young men with a coffin like box and a glittering sword. He shoved it in the box to show it was empty and then invited the girl to step inside it, placing the lid firmly on top of her. Images of the Kelly brothers flashed through my mind and there was a collective gasp as he stuck the sword straight into the middle of the box again, then cut away until it parted in two. It was then I began to feel sick. People were shouting and some women even crying. One joker called out, "And her mother just gone too!" Then, at just the right moment, the parts of the box were pushed back together, the lid raised, and the girl jumped out perfectly in one piece. Cheers and the laughter of relief followed until a last singer took Maskelyne's place. He sang Irish ballads without excuse, one even in their own language, ending on a comic one which everyone seemed to know and join in with. Then without feeling any time had passed at all – it was over.

Groups formed and chatted with a reluctance to leave, to throw off the colour, the warmth, the lights and laughter and return to the everyday world. Friends of Henry's approached us and I was introduced. Two well-dressed young men and a woman, not in the least from the lower orders and eager to discuss how the girl could have escaped being cut in half. It felt warming to be part of something for the first time since I had arrived – for the first time ever really. On our way out we each gave a penny to a collection for the family of a performer who they all seemed to have loved and who had died of consumption a few months earlier. I was reminded several times of what an act I had missed there! Outside still lively groups drifted off in different directions and Henry went off with his friends as they all lived near each other. I headed down the street my head full of the beautiful sad girl on the horse and the Greek statue until I suddenly realised that I really needed to sleep. After visiting the outhouse, I almost floated up the stairs and found a note lying on top of the gun which lay in full view on my coverlet,

"Look after this. We are watching you. Remember –
'She left them hanging out the back!'"

A cold wave prickled down my spine – he had been
watching me all the time and could enter my room with ease.
Picking the gun up, I lay back, vowing to stay awake in case
the man came back, but as my head touched the pillow a
black wave of sleep overcame me completely.

Chapter 7

Next morning I woke to find myself fully dressed upon the covers, cradling the gun like a baby. My head ached and my leg did too. Shakily I hid the gun again, this time behind the press, wrapped in a cravat, all the while feeling it was of little use when someone could find it so easily. Changing into a clean shirt, shaving in the cold water from yesterday's bowl and smoothing my hair and moustache with a few drops of Macassar, I decided a little cologne might also disguise my slept in look, then I made my way slowly down the steep stair-case.   After a chop, fried eggs and a mug of tea I began to feel much improved and set off to work – a thought which still made me smile. Back in Prickwillow, Father would have taken his early walk by the river Lark, bathed in marsh bird-song and the sound of the side lever steam engine hissing and chugging at the water levels. Mother would be at the table complaining to Bridie about the state of her one boiled egg, and Etta would be sitting opposite her, dreaming loudly of the latest lad to attract her attention, and the time when she could escape the grey and endless days that stretched ahead.

As I reached the High Street, I decided that, gun or no gun, I was happier than I had ever been in that restricted world. Trying to avoid a flock of noisy geese which crowded around my feet ended my thoughts for the moment.

Reaching the Chronicle office without much geese dropping on my shoes, I went straight in, noting that Maud was still not there, and found Caligula stretched out on my desk, idly kicking my pen nib around.

"Leave him be," called Nathaniel coming in and seeing me about to lift him, "Mr. Creed loves him in here!"

Slightly suspicious at his friendly approach, by then I should have realised what would happen next. "Thank you. Not sure I want to be scratched anyway after the battle with angry geese I've just had!"

Mr. Creed entered a few moments later and threw his hat hard at the stand. "Get that vermin out of here Vail, at once," he snapped and aimed a cunningly dodged swipe at my desk, followed by Caligula's graceful descent and slow saunter out into the hall.

"I did tell him, Mr. Creed, but he said he didn't care for your opinion of the cat," Nathaniel stated smugly.

"Well, he'll care soon enough when it comes to wages day," Creed said leaning over my desk in a threatening way.

I refused to give Nathaniel the benefit of a glance and we were soon in our morning meeting. Henry, rushing in late, was given the job of attending the inquest into the market carter's death and Nathaniel of speaking with a man who claimed to predict the weather.

"If his predictions are correct think of the value to farmers," smirked Henry, enjoying Nathaniel's scowl at the task. Finally, Mr. Creed asked me to return to Esh New Winning and report on the funeral of the two Kelly boys.

Now I knew the way, the journey was easy and there seemed to be no sign of my follower. Once there, I trailed a group of sombre looking men and women along the main street who led me straight to the church of The Blessed Virgin. Its square grey shape stood in a satisfied way amongst the stone dotted greenery of the graveyard. People were going straight in, there seemed to be no carriages or coffins to follow and nobody noticed me or questioned my presence, so I slipped into a bench near the back. Two people to my right muttered together as we waited,

"Tis a beautiful long night they've had here and so many come to watch and pray," said one.

"Aye and a long night to come for those two lads," the other replied.

I realised then that they meant the coffins and if I stood up as tall as possible I could just see, over the women's hats and the men's smoothed down hair, the shape of two boxes, thankfully covered with lids this time. Shafts of light from long narrow side windows lit on the lids and a strong smell of what I later discovered was incense irritated my nose and made my eyes sting. Then all went quiet at some unseen signal and everyone stood up at once as if on marionette strings.

For almost an hour, as the church grew hotter and the smell even stronger, the priest talked in Latin, the sound of which I had gained from Will's schoolbooks. The congregation faced the back of his head, joining in at times in a mumbled drone. I recognised communion from my Father's church and noticed that the priest was the imperious Father Lodge from outside Mrs. Kelly's house. At the end, he actually turned and faced us to give a speech about how John

Joseph and Patrick were already dressed in white and waiting around the throne of the Lord in heaven. Then his tone changed abruptly and he stepped forward, placing a hand on each coffin,

"These are two deaths that should not have happened. Where was the safety for these lads? Deaths and injury are too common here. The owners make their money on the toil of your backs and I have to tie up the ends of the horrors they allow to happen. We can all pray—but sometimes more than prayer is needed." In the dramatic pause he allowed to hang after this, two well-dressed men, top hats in hand, rose and walked swiftly out. Someone near me called out, 'Amen' and was joined by a chorus of voices.

Then, as if none of that had happened, the priest nodded to two boys swinging smoking metal objects on chains, and the coffins were picked up and carried down the aisle. Everyone began to sing in English, though it was a hymn I had never heard, and to peel out bench by bench. As the priest passed me, he nodded —he knew who I was and why I was there. Outside it was mainly women who walked to the graveside as most of the men were heading away for the next shift. I found a spot where I would not draw attention to myself and leaned thankfully against the stone church wall. There was more Latin from the priest and then a sudden wailing rose from the women, sounding both fearful and desperate. The shocking sound almost overbalanced me and I had to get away. I had enough to make an excellent story for the paper and as I headed away the wailing followed for a while, then stopped abruptly, as if a musical conductor had dropped his baton. I found myself at the tail end of the snake of men. No one noticed me or showed any reaction to my presence until a low voice spoke in my ear, spinning me round, "Running away then?"

My stomach flipped at the sight and smell of her, soap and herbs and summer grass, blue eyes twinkling a smile below her shawl covered hair.

"Don't worry, they're done now. Don't think anyone noticed we had a proddy in our midst! Walk with me," Ina commanded, and pulled my arm, leading me to the side of the track where two flat capped miners stood waiting for us.

"This is Thomas Maguire and Sean Maguire—my brothers," she indicated, introducing us.

"And this is Thadeus Vail — the newspaper writer I told you about." They nodded but ignored my outstretched hand. For a moment no one spoke, then Ina broke the silence. Looking carefully around she lowered her voice, speaking forcefully in the language she had used with her mother, then translated for me,

"They say your friend is getting involved in a dangerous game. They are ......,"but Thomas cut her off,

"Irish—born here but Irish. She's told you what we stand for —our heritage and our country. There is a plan afoot. Whatever you or your friend hear or know, we need your silence." He had moved closer to me as he spoke until his face was right in front of mine—he could have pushed me into the path of crunching boots.

"If you write anything we will know and you will not get off well. Understand?" he spoke slowly as if to a child and for a moment all I could think of was that he did not sound

Irish at all, and did not know that I had a gun myself. I nodded forcefully.

Both brothers smiled then and in the most polite and friendly manner Sean said, "Nice to meet you Thadeus, take care on your journey home. And Ina you get home quickly—Da cannot be looking after Kieran all day, he is still on the back shift!" With smiles and nods of farewell they stepped off the bank and were swallowed up into the almost finished flow of miners.

In a moment, Ina and I were alone.

"Come on, you can be my guardian knight, it's much less than an hour to get back to Cornsay. Let's not talk of those two."

The idea of anyone relying on me for safety overcame the questions I was about to ask of her. What friend of mine were they talking of, what part did they play in any secret plans? Just for that moment I could be a hero and that was all that mattered.

The day was pleasant and the idea of passing time alone again with Ina would suffice for then. Very soon she found a stile and we scrambled over into the field beyond, which ran down to a stream. I had always found flat roads easier to follow than bumped and rutted ground but when I was with Ina it seemed all the same. A few trees dotted the banks and about half-way she slipped off her shawl and spread it on the ground, insisting we rest. I leaned back against the rough trunk and felt hot sparks ignite inside me as she sat down so close her arms and dress were pressed against me. A slight breeze ruffled both our hair and ran across the skin of our faces and hands. A bird sang a long aching song nearby and the river rippled over the slippery shallows.

"You should take care of what my brothers say," Ina murmured. "They know people who could hurt you." I wanted to tell her then of the gun man and Maud but she placed her finger on her lips to quiet me. "Shh! It is peaceful here and this tree reminds me of a story I know. Can I tell it to you?"

I could only nod and try and calm my breathing to hers.

"There was a beautiful young woman named Cliodhna, a queen of the banshees. She lived on an island in the Land of Promise and kept three birds, like that one up there, who lived on the fruit of a magic tree. Their song was so sweet they could cure any ailment with it."

She paused and rested her hand on my thigh where each finger burned through to my heated skin, then continued, "One day she met and fell in love with a handsome mortal and she chose to leave the Land of Promise and become mortal herself to be with him."

The fingers began to move rhythmically as she spoke, "But the powers of the old gods were angry with her and they lured her to sleep with harp music. Then rose a terrible wave which took her and swept her away."

Then she leaned in and kissed me for the second time. Both our hearts beat faster and we breathed as if riding a wave together until, just at its height, the loud screech of the whistle from the mine broke the enchantment, and she pulled away pink and panting, "Oh no! It's the shift change!" She pulled her clothing straight and tried to tuck her wayward hair back into shape all in the same movement as she jumped to her feet. "I must get back else Da will be left with Kieran and a shift to get to. I must run. Keep following along the bank and you'll reach the road again and find the station."

Her form flew off without another word and I sat awhile, gazing up into the tree and feeling the memory of her touch until it began to grow cold.

I had to get back to Darlington and get rid of that gun somewhere no one could find it. If I stopped the signal getting to whoever was in charge of the Fenians, I could save them. The words of Ina's brothers had matched her description of what a Fenian stood for—even if they had stopped short of admitting it.

My mind had cleared and I knew what I had to do.

Chapter 8

I reached the newspaper offices that Saturday feeling as if no time had passed, ruffled Caligula's ears, and nodded to the print room boy at the desk. "No Maud?" He grunted a negative reply.

Back behind my desk, my mind drifted as an ink lake formed around my pen nib. I seemed to have lost the ability to form words and found myself smiling as I shaped the lake into a spider. Henry's noisy arrival broke into my daydream and I shook myself, grabbing the wet spider and crumpling it into the basket for waste.

"Good funeral?" Ina's touch and my quest to halt whatever was being planned, had almost pushed the Kelly boys from my mind.

"The best!" I quipped, "Plenty to write about anyway. How was the inquest—anything surprising in the result?"

Henry assumed a grave manner and spoke in the voice of an official, 'Mr. Clarke was ill and should not have been in charge of the horse and cart. Death was from angina pectoris and heart break at the death of his wife. The verdict is accidental death attributable to irresponsibility'. Then in his own voice, "The lesson here, young Thadeus, being — do not get ill in an irresponsible way!"

We laughed heartily then set to work on our articles. Mr. Creed had wanted lots of colour in my story and I gave it to him, all the time aware that I was going to reveal everything to him about the Fenians and the gun when he arrived. Nathaniel came in as we worked and threw a letter onto my table, which I was just quick enough to catch before it slipped into my wet ink.

"Well—what's the weather going to be like tomorrow then, Nat?" chuckled Henry, before I could check the handwriting on the front.

"Cold in the morning. No rain. Warmer later on. Oh, and it's Nathaniel actually, I am no smock wearing land worker myself!"

Their banter receded into the background as I opened the letter. It was from my father. My heart thudded and I felt a familiar churning in my stomach. The message was clear. Etta had run away and was nowhere to be found. They needed me to return and help search for her. I would have to ask Mr. Creed to let me go. My hand shook as I read Mother's postscript; *End this ridiculous occupation, which you have no need of, and return immediately. Your sister's and our reputation are far more important at this moment.*

Controlling my shaking with some effort I pushed the letter into my jacket pocket and stood up. Mr. Creed entered and I handed him my article.

Skim reading it as he took off his coat and threw his hat on the rack, he nodded. "Not sure about the headline—*Two boys' last journey*—but this is good, Thadeus—you are beginning to remind me why I hired you. First story page again! Well done!"

The glow that gave me was extinguished by what I had to say next.

"My father has sent me a letter Mr. Creed. I think I must go home. My sister is missing. They need me to help find her." I finished lamely.

The whole room had become silent, then to my surprise, he nodded, "Of course, your family is important. You can have one week—but after that I would have to think about replacing you. You understand?"

Relief mixed with a feeling of dread within me as if some monstrous sea creature was wrapping its tentacles around my legs and pulling me down.

"There is a late train today to the south overnight. You can go back to your lodgings and collect your possessions," commented Henry helpfully as I left.

All the way back I could only think that I hadn't told Mr. Creed about the gun and wondered whether I should take it with me. I had time to lose it completely before the train and no one would follow me to Prickwillow where knowledge of coal mines and Fenians was scant. The next letter however, changed my direction again. Mrs. Furness handed it to me as I entered the hallway, still busy with afternoon cleaning.

"This just arrived Mr. Vail —redirected from the Chronicle—I'm surprised they didn't hand it to you. I wasn't expecting to see you just yet. The maids might be in your room." Then she tutted at my rapidly disappearing back. Panting and stumbling up the narrow back stair I reached my door and opened it to find all was tidy and unoccupied. The gun was where I had left it, and I sank onto the bed with relief and opened the letter;

My dear Thadeus,

          Do not believe what they tell you. I am safe and happy. John and I are together and married. We forged Father's permission letter. It was so easy. A curate in Ely married us as he recognised Father's name! We are staying hidden for now but will go to London soon. Bridie is with us too (though she wants to be Bridget now) and we are going to live with her relatives who have work for John. Father does not know where this is so I have written it on a separate note. Do Not Tell Him or come to look for me! Please make up a story to tell them. You are so skilled at that.

Mrs. John Hill

P.S. Being in love is so wonderful—you should try it!

The letter slipped from my fingers and I slumped back onto the pillows and rubbed my eyes. John Hill—she was married to John from the farm. Father and Mother would be mortified. No comfy curate for their daughter at the appropriate age, just rolled sleeves and hard work. And real happiness. I began to smile. Etta was safe and had no need of my travelling to look for her. I pocketed the London address. I would write to our parents later but in my mind, I cut off the sea monster's tentacles. Ina and her family were more in need of my help than Etta. I would return to the Chronicle, tell Mr. Creed everything and give myself up. Once the police knew Maud was held hostage it would prove my story correct. Rehiding the gun deep in the cushions of the old chair, wrapped in a sock, I threw some of my clothes into my valise and re-traced my steps.

As I passed the market, I took the opportunity to buy a cold sausage to eat on the train to

Cornsay, and one to give Caligula. I placed them, paper wrapped and sticky, into my pocket and took the now famil-iar steps up to the Chronicle doors. Noise hit me as I en-tered. The presses had started up. I took a moment to slip the sausage to the cat and then straighten my hair and moustache in Queen Victoria's reflective glass. The valise went behind the main desk to disguise the truth of where I was actually planning to go, and I only carried my satchel. Light from the open door showed me Nathaniel ushering in a person who seemed familiar.

"Let us past, Vail," fussed Nathaniel, "This gentleman has urgent business with Mr. Creed. Why are you here any-way—aren't you off to rescue your fallen sister?"

"I left my hat," I made up quickly.

"Well, you should come in and listen then. Plenty of time before the late train south—and it's about your friends—the Irish!"

In the office Mr. Creed and Nathaniel perched on their desks and Henry and I sat behind ours. The newcomer faced them and introduced himself,

"Good day gentlemen. I am James Ward, a clerk at the Iron Works here which, as you know, employs many Irish. Whilst passing through the works the day before yesterday I overheard some information which I feel would be of great interest to you. Would you like me to continue?"

He did not look at me or Henry, focusing only on Mr.

Creed, while Nathaniel nodded sagely. Yet again I realised that my chance to reveal all about the gun had to be suppressed.

"I believe it would be of some value to the Chronicle to be the first to report on this matter as it appertains to the missing murder weapon," he continued. Creed's reply covered the strangled moan which I managed to turn into a cough.

"Ah I see! It is of financial value to you as well of course sir! If it proves to be true then why have you not spoken to the police first?" The man pulled out a large white handkerchief and blew his nose, taking his time before replying,

"I am on my way to the police next but I feel this matter is of grave importance to the wider community and you are the person to champion the cause of the people, are you not Mr. Creed?

"One guinea," snapped Creed.

The man smiled as if a polite bargain had been successfully struck and was about to continue when the editor followed it up with, "If you give me the name of the source." Much affronted, James Ward continued, "Surely that is for the police to hear first! I can only tell you what was said as I heard it."

"Very well, carry on."

"It is about the weapon used in the recent murder here. As you know, there are some troublesome Irish in this area, and some who are perfectly law abiding. The group I overheard were talking about the murder and about another violent plot being planned by the Fenians." At this point I noticed he looked carefully at Nathaniel, "A plan to cause a dangerous explosion. On the main rail tracks going north and south."

A general gasp flew around the room and a pain shot through my stomach. The gun man had said it was the signal for something to happen. That something could well be this explosion and if so, I was already involved in the plot myself. If I had spoken up then, I could save my own skin but Ina and her family may be destroyed.

I jumped to my feet and gasped that I had to take my top hat and get to the station immediately. My family were waiting for me. I couldn't tell whether I stumbled because of my fear or because Nathaniel pushed me, but I prayed that it did not give me away. I had to warn the Maguire brothers to put a stop to the horror they may be part of.

Chapter 9

It seemed to me that my life had become a succession of train journeys and surprises as I rattled along the single track to Cornsay that afternoon. The wood of the seat in front vied with the upright back behind me to deliver admonishing blows to my knees and shoulders. Smoke and ashes blew in through the loose fitting window and the now familiar smell of the pits grew stronger with each stop.

I had no idea of how I could get to Ina without her family discovering me, but I had to try. For some reason the image of the girl cut in half in the magician's box kept coming back to me. Sometimes Ina, sometimes Etta, changing with the churning iron wheels. Cornsay was the same as when I had first seen it. Houses stretched away from the pit in their sloping slide and the smell of wood burning from stove and fireplaces mixed with the rotten eggs of the coke and brick kilns. People were about — chatting, fetching water from the central pump and busy on everyday errands. Setting off down Ina's street, I was wary of little Kieran running out again as there were some children playing in knots, but no horse and cart to entice him. Two or three groups of gossips stopped their chatter as I passed and watched me silently.

Just as I reached the house Ina bolted out and grabbed

my hand, "Don't speak. Just walk quickly with me now," she commanded and set off down the hill to the beehive shapes. I followed as best I could until we turned into a lane behind the houses further along. Leaning against the nearest yard wall, I caught my breath. "It was in the paper, wasn't it?" I gasped. She nodded.

"It's bad, Thadeus. They've come down from Newcastle – O'Mahon and Walsh – and they are fierce angry! The boys are on shift, Da too – there's no way they can come outbye now – we have a little time. But they're looking for you! Why did you write that stuff – you promised you wouldn't?"

"Would you believe me if I said it wasn't me?"

"I might, but they won't!"

"How was it in the Chronicle already? I was there – the presses were running when the informant came in. I heard it all and that's why I came to warn you!"

She sighed in exasperation, "Stop Press! You must have heard of Stop Press!"

My knees were beginning to turn to jelly and my hands shook in a very unheroic way.

"They really believe I told the paper everything? What can I do? How can I convince them?"

"They want to speak to you – perhaps if you tell them what really happened, they might let you go!" For a moment I saw a glimmer of hope.

"They haven't got me, have they – no one but you knows I'm here." Ina looked down at our feet and said nothing. It took a moment for the silence of her reply to sink in.

"You told them, didn't you? They know where we are." When she looked up, her gaze went past me to the two dark coated men turning the corner and coming swiftly up behind me.

"Many thanks, Miss Maguire," one of them said mockingly. "We'll look after your friend from here. With us – you!" and without touching me, they crowded either side and set a pace for the kilns. I did not look back. We approached a wooden shed a little way further on from the last brick beehive. I tried to ask them what it was they wanted or to explain that it wasn't me, but the only reply I got was a poke in the ribs and a terse, "Shut up now!"

Like a tender lamb, I wasn't prepared for the blow to my head or the darkness that followed.

After a time, which could have been an hour or a whole night, I returned suddenly to the light. Gritty earth grazed my ear and cheek and pain radiated out into a thumping agony across my skull. The smell of the brick kilns and smoke from burning tobacco mixed with the muffled mumbling of two voices. I held myself there a little longer, even though my knees and elbows cried out for movement. If I kept still as long as possible, I hoped they might leave me for dead. A groan of pain escaped my control as the thudding in my skull turned into a strong urge to be sick. One of the voices exclaimed in Ina's language and rough hands pulled me up into a sitting position as my top hat was thrust onto my lap.

"Use that!" it almost chuckled in English. So, I did, swallowing the sour aftertaste in choking coughs. They were both sitting on crates close to me, one candle lighting the gloom. One was all legs and arms, dark curls haloing his face, the other an older man, greying spikes to his balding pate. Neither looked like a murderer, but I was beginning to learn just how hard it was to tell. The younger one spoke, leaning awkwardly forward,

"Right! Tell us how the hell you're involved in all this!" Not sure what they might do next, I gasped between coughs,

"I told no one—about the Fenian plot I mean. I promised Ina I wouldn't – It wasn't me!" I strangled a yell as the older man landed his boot on my knee.

"Who was it then? Not Ina surely?" he followed with. But the name of the dapper clerk in Mr. Creed's office escaped me even in the fear of another kick.

"The signal — I know about that —and I've not told anyone." This time the older man spoke very quietly and without the use of violence.

"What signal?"

So, the first time I told all about the gun man, Maud, and the notes was to McMahon and Walsh in the hut near the brick kilns. They seemed enlivened by the information and discussed it for a while as if it solved the riddle of a long held puzzle. I took the chance to sit up further and place the hat of vomit on the floor beside me. They finished and McMahon, who I had now worked out was the older man, got as close to my face as he could.

"Listen son, this is very important for our cause. That gun is a sign. When you bring it here and give it to the cell leader, he will pass it on. Can we trust you to get it and bring it back?" I felt a rush of anger spark through me and make my head thud even more.

"Why should I? I could be caught as the murderer from Darlington— or at least his accomplice. I could be sent to prison for treason!"

"Or hung of course!" pointed out Walsh. A long look passed between them then.

"Let's put it this way Mr. Vail—you will do it!" McMahon said gruffly. "Ina Maguirre will go with you and make sure you return —or we will have to exact a forfeit from her. You can imagine how that might be!" They stood up, filling the little shed with their height, "First train in the morning. We'll lock you here 'til then just to be sure. Oh, and tidy yourself up by the way — what a stink!"

I winced as Walsh aimed a kick at my other knee but stopped just before he connected. They replaced their large caps and left, bolting the door outside as they did. As it shot home the name of the informer suddenly came to me from somewhere and I shouted after them,

"James Ward—that was his name, from the forge!" I wasn't sure they heard me as their footsteps faded, one of them whistling tunefully as they went.

After an attempt at standing I gave in to the spinning of my head and stomach and slumped back onto the ground. I seemed to have become more and more deeply involved in this mess, to the point where my pantry hiding place in Prickwillow and Bridie's warm arms called to me strongly. Drifting in and out of reality for a while eased my head a little, though the smell of vomit grew stronger than the brick kiln haze. I had no idea how much time had passed when I woke to find hands touching my hair and flinched away.

"Stay still cara—I'm nearly done," murmured Ina. Struggling awake, I pulled at her arm.

"What do you want? You're one of them—you betrayed me!" I cried, my voice sounding like a high wail as my anger spilled over. Very calmly, she finished tending to my head and sat back on her heels.

"There's no saying no to them—I warned you! For Thomas and Sean's sake I have to do what I'm told. I'm only a woman. Why did you not tell me about the gun and your friend?"

"I did! I mean I came down to tell you—but things took over, didn't they?"

Ina became practical, collecting up the cloths and the bowl she had come in with and preparing to toss my hat out into the field. Then she left. My anger evaporated with her going; whatever happened I couldn't let them hurt her. Dozing again it only seemed to be moments before she came back, empty handed, and sat down beside me. We didn't speak for a while then, she said,

"Your head's not too bad now I can see. Tomorrow we have to go to Darlington together. Ma thinks I'm staying with my sister Ailis and her family for the night."

The checks on her bodice seemed to become minutely clear to me then, even in the dim light, the buttons cascading down like logs over a waterfall. Lace at her neck moved slightly with each breath and her pale face took shadows from the dark around. I pulled her to me to kiss. She placed my hand over her small round breast and her own hands held my face.

"Remember the banshee!" I groaned

"And the beautiful birds" she laughed, as we set ourselves free.

Later, we dressed each other and talked until sleep overcame us. When I woke it was dawn and I was alone. Grey light filtered through the cracks between the wooden boards and the movement of sitting up started a drumming in my skull. The bolt slid across on the door and the latch rattled as I tried to organise my thoughts and Ina slid around it. I made an effort to spread the aches I felt evenly around my body. Wherever there was a muscle there seemed to be an ache.

"It's time! We have half an hour before the first train up to Durham—how is your head?"

"Much improved," I lied, "but Ina do you—did we.....?" I trailed off.

Smiling, she bent down towards me but instead of the kiss I was expecting she just checked the back of my head and helped me to my feet. "It's a new day, cara—we must be gone!"

Once I was upright the shed seemed to have shrunk and I let the dizziness wash over me for a few seconds before we both stepped outside. The walk up to the station woke me even further and we got onto an empty wooden carriage which rattled us up to Durham. Ina was quiet and I had little energy, so we shared a silence while I ran through all the different scenarios that could be waiting for us in Darlington, and whether the gun would still be there at all.

Chapter 10

Once on the main line train, our awkwardness mellowed a little and Ina produced a cap to replace my top hat which she tried on at different angles, laughing at how ridiculous she could make herself look.

The market was dressed in its Sunday quiet. Only the baker was open and we bought bread rolls to break our fast, washing them down later with water from a nearby fountain. We found a step to sit on and watch the light stretch slowly across the grey buildings and over the sleeping cobbles. A few people, dressed for the day in their Sunday best, began to appear and stroll past us towards the early service in the old church nearby. I had no desire to be too early at my lodgings, so we followed them into the green of the graveyard and made out that we were earnestly looking for someone in particular amongst the newly gleaming rows of stones.

"I wonder if I will get so shiny a stone to mark my grave," Ina wondered. "Look here, this girl was my age, only eighteen — not old enough to have married or to have loved." I remember I had wanted to tell her I would give her a beautiful memorial when the time came, but she pulled away to kneel down, exclaiming over a small angel which said 'Charles Sewell – Aged 1 year' at its base and nothing else. A shiver ran across my shoulders as I saw again Mother kneeling at just such a grave in Ely, her face grim under the black lace bonnet, ignoring the live twin watching her from behind Bridie's skirts.

"Come on, leave him! It's time to get that gun," I muttered, pulling at her shoulder a little roughly. She shook me off insisting on saying a prayer for the child, then crossed herself and rose to follow me. As luck would have it no one was passing to see her make the gesture as we would certainly have been ejected. Heading up the hill on the other side of the market from the Chronicle offices we entered the nearest yard through its archway. It opened out in the now familiar way, surrounded by the doorways to the dwellings which were mostly open, though there was no well. Children already hung about in groups and some of them surrounded us asking for money as well as our names and where we were going. I tried to push them away and move on, hoping if we ignored them they would not follow us. Ina had stopped and spoke to them in the language she had used with her mother, which sent them scurrying back into one of the doorways.

"What did you tell them?" I asked in surprise as she took my arm and hurried me on.

"Only that you are a Sidhe lord who has cast a spell on me to be your servant and you would come for them next now you know where they live!" I wasn't too sure about frightening the urchins but I found myself liking the idea of having the strength of a powerful Sidhe lord. Without looking back we walked out into the street and headed past the grocer's shop where I had first been given directions and up to the new houses where my lodgings waited. On the way I explained that she would not be allowed to enter the building.

"So, no Irish then?"

"Of course not — women are far worse a threat in the house whatever their ancestry."

"Oh, I agree there, Mr. Vail!" she replied in a stern voice which was surprisingly close to that of Mrs. Furness. I knew we were going to have to take care in retrieving the gun and somehow make sure no one was watching the place. A few people knew I had it by then and if I was caught, the police could lock me up as an accomplice to the murder and the plot. Or perhaps McMahon and Walsh, or maybe even Thomas and Sean Maguirre, would finish me off before I could talk.

The street and land around Linden House had not been fully developed at that time and wooden scaffolding clung on to walls of red brick, standing silent for a Sunday. Before we reached the growing street, we came to an area of trees and scrub land where a rough path led across towards another main thoroughfare and we stopped for a moment, finding a bank to sit on and work out our plan of action. There was no knowing if someone had already been in and retrieved the gun. As we sat, a nursemaid passed us pushing a carriage, followed by a small boy in knickerbockers and a tight looking tweed jacket. They stared quite openly at us and with a sudden urge to hide our faces, I turned to Ina and kissed her. I heard the child laughing as his nursemaid pulled him swiftly on, until Ina pushed me away and gasped, "Hiding our faces? You are becoming a proper plotter Thadeus! Perhaps we should continue—it doesn't seem to have put *her* off staring

— that woman over there!" She pointed to a young woman in sober dress, hair piled smartly under a jaunty velvet hat which trailed a brown feather from its crown. At Ina's interest, she approached hurriedly down the path,

"Thadeus! Thadeus Vail! It *is* you! Where have you been? They said you had gone home to Norfolk!" It was Maud Lemon—looking fine, healthy and quite safe.

Ina held onto my arm as Maud approached, making it slightly difficult to rise and raise my hat, so I had to push her firmly off. Maud looked well turned out and if anything, better than when I had first met her, dispelling the images I had had of her wasting away in a dark cell or at least pacing a locked room in a helpless manner.

"But why are you here? Shouldn't you be rescuing your sister from certain ruin? I've just been into the office – it was the talk of Henry, Nathaniel and the print room boys!"

"What happened to you? You were never there —he said you were held against your will..." My questions rushed out, falling over each other until Ina cut in with,

"Good day to you, Madam. I am Ina, Ina Maguire", and held out her hand for Maud to shake. She introduced herself and suggested we all sit down on the bank and explain ourselves. She began. She did not work every day, only filling in occasionally. Mr. Creed was her uncle and she was working with him to become the first female reporter. The day I had arrived she had left me, quite safely, and travelled to a village called Croft, where she had been requested to attend her aunt (her mother's sister not Mrs. Creed), whose illness seemed to be taking a long time to heal, even though there were little outer signs of it. Several days had passed in endless games of 'Twenty Questions', whist and ecarte and long sessions of hearing Maud read passages mainly from the Bible. I started to try and explain all that had happened with me when Ina jumped to her feet and interrupted firmly,

"We have little time left — the signal remember—that's why we are here, Thadeus!" She leaned down and jerked my arm, pulling me up and setting the pain alight again in my head.

"Wait!" Maud joined us. "I came here yesterday before going into the Chronicle. I thought we could walk in together. I saw Nathaniel—I think it was him anyway—leaving in a hurry, so I called and a maid told me you had gone away. She knew nothing else but I heard it all when I got to the office of course. A man had visited Nathaniel there. Henry told me they had talked in the hallway not realising he was listening behind the open door. He overheard most of it. There is a police spy at the Forge rooting out Fenians and he is some relative of Nathaniel's. They are using you, Thadeus — something about a signal and trying to discover who the leaders are. If you do what they want you cannot win. Leave whatever this signal is and escape to Norfolk until it all blows over."

For a moment, we all fell silent. Trees fluttered gently in the breeze and a horse and carriage rattled by in the distance.

"Nathaniel?" I finally asked.

"He set you up even before you arrived. I thought if you'd left for Ely you would be safe for now. I came up here to try and get your family's address and send a letter to warn you."

Ina had remained silent but then muttered almost to herself at first, "Thomas, Sean, Da —we have to hurry, Thadeus, before McMahon triggers what they have in mind. If we get back today we can find Da and persuade him to lose the gun—not let anyone know he had it. There'll be other times and they won't use you again."

"Your father's the Fenian leader—not Thomas and Sean?"

"You have a gun?" Maud and I exclaimed at once.

Ina took my hand her eyes pleading, "We have it in our power to put a stop to all of this and save a lot of people. Please get the gun and we can get back to Da today. If he does not agree to get rid of it, then we can."

The thought of McMahon and Walsh and the retribution they would take on Ina if we did was enough to strengthen my resolve. Maud, who seemed to have become excited by the intrigue of it all, agreed to go around the front of Linden House and observe any comings and goings, while Ina and I headed to the lane which ran between the street and a big grey stone church. There was a gate set into the red bricks of the wall next to the opening for coal deliveries which was luckily unlocked and we pushed it open, shooting the bolt across behind us. Ina pulled her dark shawl over as much of her face as she could and pressed herself against the back wall of the house where she couldn't be seen from any of the windows. We didn't speak as I lifted the latch gently on the scullery door and slipped inside. From there, I needed to enter the kitchen which should be empty on a Sunday morning and cross the stone tiles to the big swing servants' door. Heat from the blackened range burning permanently in the chimney space hit me, but first glance showed no one was present. A purple slab of beef waited on the table, kept company by cold pans of floating vegetables and a marbled plate of shiny lard. The big door would slam noisily unless I held it, which was difficult without any handles, but I thought I had got safely through without alerting anyone until a voice called out,

"Sermon boring was it?" It came from the lodgers' parlour behind the first door on my right and I froze.

"I thought you must be away somewhere as you were not at breakfast. I'm so sick I stayed away from the service," sniffed an extra mucous dripping Jim, as he came out of the parlour and sneezed noisily into my face.

"I saw you through the door jam," he muttered into a large grubby blue handkerchief. "Your friend left you this—said you would know what to do about it." He handed me a folded note, then leaned against the door frame as if waiting for more information.

"What friend — er, I mean what did he look like? I have a lot of friends here," I ended somewhat lamely.

"Well, if you read it you'll see, won't you?" Jim nodded encouragingly. So I did.

Take signal to Esh Winning. Place in bag under bench at station. We are watching.

Struggling not to show Jim that my heart was racing and stomach churning, I forced my face into what I hoped would pass for a pleasantly surprised grin,

"How nice! He wants to meet for a stroll later. I must hurry and get back to church. I forgot my Book of Common

Prayer and I prefer to use my own—not one of those grubby communal ones!"

"Aye! You never know what you might catch," he observed before another sneezing fit. "Have a good pray then!" before wandering back to his seat beside the lodgers' fire.

I was absurdly conscious of time passing by then. I felt it crawling over my skin and speeding my breathing as I mounted the front stairs and crossed the first landing to the little door which led me back onto my own steep treads and up to my open bedroom door. I could see the gun clearly from there. It had been taken out and nestled like an infant in the middle of the eiderdown as if it hadn't already taken a life and was about to signal the possible removal of many more. Stepping inside the room, I picked it up with care and placed it back into the bag it came in, pushing it down into my satchel before turning back and heading down to the kitchen and out into the yard to collect Ina. But she was gone. I could not have called her in case someone was close by watching but before panic took over I heard a loud hiss,

"Thadeus, come out!" and the gate latch rattled as it opened. Ina had seen a person come out of the house and cross the yard swiftly without looking back. She thought whoever it was had not seen her but had left the yard in case they returned. From my description she agreed it was not Jim and we both felt a coldness.

If not Jim, then who was it? The service was in full swing in the church on the other side of the lane and strains of 'My hope is built on nothing less' filled the air. There seemed to be nobody watching— but by then I was realising that these people were exceptionally good at concealment.

Chapter 11

Maud met us around the front and promised to put Nathaniel off the track when she went into the Chronicle in the morning—although it seemed it may have been a little late for that by then. The gun bounced against my hip in the satchel and my limp was affecting my gait, along with the exhaustion and headache which were both growing worse. We walked a longer, more roundabout way through yards and alleys to reach the station. Maud had pointed them out to us. Thankfully Ina made no comment, just quietly threading her arm through mine for support.

Once there, I was disappointed to discover that there were few trains on the Sabbath and we must wait an hour for the next. Men and women could not wait together so we had to separate or remain standing on the platform. We had bought and eaten a cold pie from a stall just outside and I needed to sit and rest. If I had sunk down on the ground, my dishevelled appearance could well have had us thrown out as beggars or vagrants. My moustache and hair had begun to curl in an unruly manner and a rough beard was beginning, as well as the smell of someone who had not washed for a while. All of that and my cloth cap belied my status, but luckily no one was in the gentlemen's waiting room so I took the chance to drift off on one of the hard wooden benches where I had lain on first arriving in Darlington, which seemed like a lifetime ago. In my jumbled dream I was climbing the scaffolding beside Linden House escaping from a pursuer I could not see but I knew was Will. When I looked down, I seemed to be at a great height and I knew that the only way to avoid capture was to jump—so I stepped off into thin air. As I fell, my foot kicked out and I was awake again, heart racing and feeling for the safety of the gun in my satchel. I had only a moment to enjoy the relief of solid ground when a railway employee opened the door and leaned in shouting, 'Next one North—five minutes'. Jumping up, I followed him and found Ina just outside.

"Thank God you are alright! I was outside and could hear you shouting. I thought you may be under attack!"

"Only a dream," I reassured myself as well as Ina before our words were lost to the rattle and hiss of the approaching engine.

The one for Esh was waiting at Durham this time and we secured an empty section for ourselves, ready to be rattled into the coal fields again. Just as it was about to roll, two latecomers came running down the ramp and I jumped back towards Ina when I recognised them. It was Nathaniel and the gun man.

"It's them – they got on. A couple of carriages down!" I gasped.

"They can't change carriages and the only stop on Sunday is Esh Winning so we'll have to get off before then and make a run for it."

"How—how can—?"

"It always slows right down where the wagonways cross just before Esh. We can jump."

I was struck silent for a few moments at the thought of something so dangerous.

"We can do it—just jump away from the wheels so it doesn't hit us when it picks up speed again," Ina explained, seeming to think little of the effort it would take me to land safely.   "Look, Thadeus—it's not the gun they're after you know, or even you—they want to catch whoever comes for it. It's my Da. He will come and they will get him. You've got to save him!"

"Your father is the local leader—the one who wants to blow us up to get his country back?" I was stunned.

"Please Thadeus—I will explain. I want it all to stop. To get to him before they do and beg him to stop. We're beginning to slow now. Get ready!" She did not hesitate. "It will not stand still, so keep running. They are not expecting us to escape with the gun so it will give us a head start!" Her last words were obscured by a cloud of smoke— then she jumped.

The train pulled into a slow slide and I took a deep breath and followed her onto the cinder track. Perhaps it was the thought of capture or perhaps the thought of falling under the big iron wheels but I managed to land on my feet in the smoky confusion. I hoped I was heading in Ina's direction as I ran. Next moment, a hand thrust out of the haze towards me and I grabbed it. It pulled me away from the track bed, over a low fence of some sort and Ina's voice hissed in my ear, "Get down and stay down!"

I rolled onto a patch of soggy grass and pressed myself into it as the engine picked up speed and disappeared on its noisy way. As the smoke cleared I struggled upright, adding mud and grass stains to my already dishevelled appearance. Beside me, Ina was flushed with what seemed like a combination of exertion and excitement. "We don't have much time before they realise we are not at Esh Winning" she panted, "We need to find a place to hide."

My heart sank—not again! "But we are here. We could leave the gun and when no one comes to pick it up after we've warned your Da he is being watched, then we are all free."

She sighed and rolled her eyes—I thought a little too dramatically.

"Thadeus don't you see—then you and I will be arrested. You have been holding the gun for them all this time. And McMahon and Walsh will come back for me whatever happens. I think we should keep the gun with us while I go and find Da and talk to him. He might not agree with us of course so then we will have to think of another plan, for they will all be looking for us!"

She stood up and looked around.

"Come on, we must get to Cornsay Colliery quickly—they will not look for us there straight away. We have a bit of time."

I did not speak for a while as we headed for the grey brooding church and then down to the river-bank where I had heard the story of Cliodhna the banshee. Late summer had still not quite taken the green from the tree as we passed it but the afternoon was drawing in with a nip. No lazing on the bank this time; we hurried on without a backward glance. My head still ached and the knowledge that Nathaniel has set me up before I had even left Prickwillow and knew about the gun and Maud's freedom, was churning inside it. Even Ina had been duping me—allowing me to believe her brothers were a danger when actually her father was more so to me and possibly to many other people. I wondered when not telling all that one knows becomes a lie in itself. An unformed thought also fluttered around my head like a summer white butterfly. Perhaps the Irish were actually as bad as the newspapers had reported. We reached the stile and stood at the bottom of Cornsay Colliery. If Ina had turned and leaned in to kiss me then I would have forgiven her everything of course.

As we walked, she tried to explain more.

"Da will tell you his story when we talk to him. It will help explain a lot of it. The Fenians talk a lot you know but as far as I have any knowledge of their workings this is the first time they have planned any action."

"Action! That is what my brother used to say—he was 'going into action'. It meant fighting. Fought his way to a painful death in the end!"

We had taken an unfamiliar street and were approaching an area of land that was laid out for growing what looked like vegetables. A wooden shed stood at the back of it and a few men worked patches digging, watering and pulling plants to place in barrows. Ina stopped and pulled me back, "Oh, there's Ben Martyn—Da's marrow—his work mate—he must not see me. He's from Cornwall and no Fenian, but he will tell him I was with a stranger."

We doubled back and took a longer lane behind a street to reach an arched opening, quietly dark for the day which Ina explained was one route into an adit, the entrance to a mine, which opened at ground level. A rail track led into its open mouth but all were resting at that time, ready to be filled with men and trucks in the early hours of Monday. Two of the wagons were standing empty and black with coal dust at the side of the tracks.

"I need you to wait here. There's a gap behind that brick building there where you can hide—or you could climb into one of those wagons. I have to talk to Da alone, then I will bring him straight here, we can get rid of the gun if he agrees and then you will be free. Please Thadeus!" She did kiss me then, and that and the way she said my name, undid any resolve to argue I had been beginning to form.

The gap was dark and home to spiders, cinders and more coal dust but we found a few wooden crates which I could sit on and at least I felt safe from discovery for the first time that Sunday. I took out my notebook and pencil, deciding to write something and possibly chronicle all that had happened so far, although little light penetrated between the wall and the building. Absently I found myself doodling small pictures instead. Beautiful Cliodha sinking in the huge waves and a huge horse standing at the tunnel's entrance. I was just starting on a tall hero to stand beside it when I heard a noise coming from the paved yard. I could only freeze and listen. Whoever was coming made no attempt to hide the noise of their boot steps and my hand slipped down to the gun, intending to use it as a threat if I needed to. At first I could only see the shape of a hooded head and a long dark garment, then I caught a ragged breath as the figure laughed and Ina said, "Oh dear—you weren't thinking of shooting me, were you?"

I felt quite angry for a moment. "I was not expecting you back so soon. Where is he?" I snapped.

"He's not there. Gone on one of his rambles over the fell— might not be back until late." She pulled up a crate and sat down. "Here, I got some food from Ma and even a jar of tea. Said I was going to help Mr. Martyn and then stay at Ailis' house the night. It's not dark yet, just seems it in here!" As we ate we discussed what to do.

"Will you stay here with me then?" I asked somewhat hopefully but her plan did not involve a repeat of the night in the shed near the brick kilns.

"As soon as it gets dark the miners will go home or to the inn or even church some of them. Many of them have to be up for an early morning shift and this place will be heaving by four. Once it's clear we can take you to the hut behind the vegetable rows. You can sleep there for a few hours and I will bring Da when he gets up the morning. He's not on the first shift. I need him to agree to getting rid of the signal and stopping the attack on the rail lines before he meets you or can get his hands on the gun."

My admiration for her was beginning to grow and her bravery was impressive. I realised I felt safer when she was around. If she had been a man she would have made a fine leader in anything she turned her hand to. I began to believe the plan could work if Mr. Maguire was half as resourceful as his youngest daughter.

Chapter 12

In his dream, Michan floats on a lake. There is no snow or ice and he feels warm and safe. He knows this place but it's different. He can see a boat in the distance and knows the fairies have sent it in the way you know things in a dream. As a Sidhe boat, it must contain the dead. As he watches it approach he knows who it must carry—but it is not them. There are only two figures floating and he is disappointed, not sad. The one facing him wears a heavy coat which he recognises but cannot place and he smiles at Michan and waves. The other facing away has a head of fair hair and begins to slowly turn towards him when he suddenly becomes afraid. He knows they must not speak or he will be dragged to the fairy rath forever and he puts out his hand, his voice cracking,

"No Kieran, no! Do not turn! Do not—" as Mary's voice is added to his, "Kieran will you leave y' Da alone now! Kieran!"

He wakes fully to find his youngest son's fingers tracing the line of his beard, eyes like saucers,

"No, Da—no shout! Wake up!"

He sits up, shaking away the last of sleep and pulls the

child to him, humming a few lines of a jig the boy loves and they both laugh at the sound of the chorus.

"'Tis happy you are now, the both of you?" smiles Mary.

Michan lifts little Kieran down to the floor and gets out of bed himself. He and Mary push it up together into its frame and then move the table across, while the child pulls his wooden horse and cart around twisting dangerously between their legs. It is still quite early and they carry on with their well-worn morning tasks. Michan takes Kieran out to the earth closet and the pump at the bottom of the lane, where they fill two cans of water, one for cooking, and one for washing and carry them back to Mary. They wash in the small yard where the tin bath is kept, then sit at the table, Kieran in the wooden chair which lifts him high. Mary finishes porridge for them all and spoons it into bowls. She will fry eggs and ham for Thomas and Sean when their shift is done.

Even though he does these things so often, Michan finds himself taking joy in all of them today. The satisfying clunk of the bed folding into place, ripples of light on the water in the pails, the firmness of his son's little fingers as he washes them and Mary's shape as she moves about the stove. They sit to eat each side of Kieran, Mary using a rag to skilfully avoid porridge from his waving spoon. Even this, which often annoys Michan, sits fine with him today. He intends to walk to Esh Winning and back this morning and collect the signal from its hiding place. On the way, he will work out a plan of what to do with it and he reaches into his pocket with his free hand, turning the blue fairy stone round and round before singing another snatch of the fairy song to his sticky son.

The child is mesmerised by it and stops eating to try and sing along.

"Michan Maguire—away with you! Ben Martyn asked if you would get to the allotment and help him this morning and I have enough to do here without cleaning porridge off the floor!" Mary is laughing as she says this. Her husband seems happier than in a long while and she doesn't want to change it. "Hadaway up there then! Ina and I must start on the wash this morning." As she says this, she feeds Kieran the last spoonfuls of his breakfast and hooks him out of the chair, almost dropping the wriggling form as Michan stands and plants a kiss on her mouth.

"I'll be away then." He blushes, surprising himself too.

Mary, already busy with other things, calls, "Oh, and knock at Ailis and Kevin's and get that lazy girl up and home please."

He goes out the back gate and heads up the lane where some women have already got their washing out. A figure moves fast towards him, skirts lifted and shawl falling back off her flaming curls.

"Da, Da!" Ina calls, "I need to speak with you now! It is life and death!"

"Slow down daughter—the wash is not that bad!"

Out of breath she reaches him, "It's about the signal—you know, the signal!"

Suddenly the light seems to have left the day. He looks around, hoping no one has heard them and hisses, "How—what—where—?"

"Walk along with me and listen please, Da. Pretend we are having a happy chat. Laugh and smile now and again."

Her tale is almost as fanciful as one of his from the old country but he finds they are heading to the vegetable plot anyway. He should have known the police would have informers—they always had in the past. Less than ten years ago, those brothers swinging alive under that Salford arch, first martyrs to the Fenian cause, were testament to that. He should have left then. He had felt strong and purposeful when it was just meetings in The Oddfellows Arms. Talking about his hurting country had brought it alive again and sharing that with others had kept him positive for its future during many long dark shifts. It had taken his mind off fire-damp, choke-damp and the rising water beneath him.

"We have the signal safe here, Da—did you understand everything? Thadeus is here with it." She opens the door of the shed where the miners store tools for gardening and gently pushes him in, closing it behind them. The darkness smells of warm wood, onions and unwashed human. A figure rises awkwardly up off the floor and stretches, attempting to brush itself down in the cramped space as Michan reaches over and pulls down the sacking cover from the small window. As light filters, in he begins to make him out. Slightly taller than himself, hair a light brown sticking out around a pale face dotted with stubble and what would have been an impressive moustache if he looked after it. He is wearing what looks like an expensive jacket which has seen better days and is rooting around in a leather satchel attempting to pull out a smaller cloth bag.

Ina opens her mouth to speak as the moment seems to hang there waiting,

"Thadeus, this is—"

"Mr. Maguire—I know. It is a relief to finally meet you, Sir," is said in an accent Michan has rarely heard, "This is the signal."

He takes it in both hands, then slipping off its cover he finds the weight and shape of a gun glinting there. "A gun! A fucking gun!" he exclaims and much to Thadeus and Ina's puzzlement, he begins to laugh. They are interrupted by the door rattling as someone tries to enter the cramped space and a voice calls, "Mick will y' move and let me in, for God's sake!"

All three look at each other, then Michan shoves the gun as deep as he can into his jacket pocket and indicates with a finger to his lips for the other two to stay silent. Opening the door, he makes a noisy fuss of bustling out and greets Ben Martyn loudly, steering him away towards the waiting bed of carrots.

"Aw! C'mon man—you are late and we've little time now before shift. What needs doing today?"

Puzzled, Ben points out the last of the row of carrots, "Well, they need pulling but we could leave them a little longer. I thought you were not coming too! Just need to put this trowel back in the shed and we can head home to get our gear."

Beyond them, the tall chimneys of the colliery belch and the noises of machinery and rattling engines stir smoke and ash into the air. Michan slaps his forehead in mock surprise, "Would you know it — I've put me cap down in there — here give us the trowel. I'll stick it back on the shelf." He is beginning to enjoy his acting ability and easily convinces Ben to set off home as he takes the tool and opens the door just enough to get in. Ina and Thadeus look like they have not moved at all, and he sees for the first time that they are of an age and very comfortable in each other's company.

"I want no violence. This—" he pats his pocket, "is going to disappear. I will pretend it never came and I have orders to call off the action if McMahon and Walsh come back sniffing. I'm off to my shift now so I think it's time for you, Mr. Vail, to set off for the next train. If you tell no one about me then Ina will be safe—I can arrange that." As he manoeuvres round to open the door again, he stops for a moment, "Oh and thanks it is to you and yours, lad. Blessings of God be upon you!" They watch him go, chuckling slightly and occasionally touching his pocket as he takes care to avoid any plants.

Even though he has a nagging doubt about Ina and the young man, Michan is still feeling happy and notices that he hasn't coughed in a while, though as soon as the thought crosses his mind it starts, causing him to stop and catch his breath. Back at the house, the boys are already in and scrubbing each other over the tin bath in the yard while Kieran wetly jumps in the puddles they are making. Mary is angrily cooking for them.

"She has never come home, Michan—the wash will have to wait now!"

He finds he is still enjoying making up tales, "Oh sorry cara—she is helping Ailis with little Eliza. She was not well with the sickness again—Ailis that is—not Eliza," he tails off, knowing that Mary will forgive her eldest daughter anything. He pulls on his boots for the mine and picks up his tin of black bread and cheese to eat in the dark later. "She will be here soon, she says." As he finishes he rises to kiss Mary on the cheek to try and cool her anger even more, though he knows that does not always work. He calls and waves 'Slán' to Thomas and Sean as they dry off and dress, then leaves by the street door. Alone for a few moments he opens the bait tin and takes out the bread, pushing it into his pocket and replacing it with the gun. Then he hurries on to catch up with Ben and the growing group of miners on their way to the pit calling, "Hey lads! Wait then!"

At the mine, he piles his jacket and cap with the others in the shelter and the overseer clocks them in. There is no long drop in a rickety cage here as it is a drift, but the men have to take care to keep out of the way of the tubs as they move up and down the slope into the hillside. He remembers tales he had heard from older miners when he had first started the work. Little children dragging and pushing them empty and full, some only six years old, guarding the fire doors down in the thick dark and women, barely dressed in the heat of the earth, roped to carts. Now they only work the pit top and the children are all over ten. He has never found where the Sidhe might be but thinks this is because the mines are not natural places but made by men digging. He always hopes those children who have died down here and the men and women too can find their way to the fairy raths somehow.

The men reach an area where the track opens out and he goes to find his place. At three feet it's higher than some he has worked and he can walk bent over in the first bit of the tunnel. Ben is following him and they both set down not far from each other and begin to chip away at the shining black rock. After a few hours and several coughing fits, they stop for their meal. Michan leans back against the sharpness of the tunnel wall and eats the cheese and the squashed block of bread, feeling the grit crunch between his teeth. He washes it down with beer from his tin flask and chats with Ben, who is only visible by the white skin surrounding his eyes where he has rubbed them to see. When they start to work again they cannot talk so he surveys the adit in his mind, searching for a place to leave the signal.

Time loses any shape down in the dark and he is surprised when the shift is over and they crawl back out to the place where they can stand. He is behind Ben on the way out and is able to find the sloping water outlet he has chosen and set the gun in its bag away to slip and float somewhere towards the open fell. Perhaps it will catch a stream out there and then a wide river and the sea itself, perhaps it will find a little cove in the darkness to nestle undisturbed forever. He touches the blue stone in his pocket and commends it to the Sidhe. Outside in the light he has been set free too and the air feels fresher on his face than it has in many years.

Chapter 13

My arrival back in Darlington that day felt in some ways like entering a black tunnel. I believed I had said good-bye to Ina forever and I knew the events involving Nathaniel and the police informer could already have been reported. I had no idea whether officers would be waiting for me at the Chronicle offices or at my lodgings. All I wanted was to retrieve my valise, bathe away the last few days and sleep. It was lunch time when I reached the market and I saw Nathaniel and Mr. Creed leaving together. They seemed deep in an animated conversation and did not stop at the chop house, rushing on at a pace past the inn we usually frequented. I had hoped Maud would be on the desk but it was a young print room apprentice, so I had to dissemble.

He looked up from whatever he was reading and smirked, "You're back already — rescued your fallen sister then?"

I could not summon the strength to admonish him. "Just hand me the valise from down there near your feet please."

"Oh, it's yours — just a bit smelly and squashed then," he said, as he evicted Caligula from the top where he seemed to have made a nest. The beast strolled to the middle of the floor just under the Queen and fixed me with a pure green glare before nonchalantly dipping his head and applying a rough pink tongue to his rear end. The lad's chuckle echoed in my ears as I tried to make an angry but dignified exit.

Back at Linden House, work was in noisy progress on the building next door and I found Mrs. Furness in the kitchen preparing a slippery pile of white offal for our evening meal. On asking for some hot water she told me that there was a small room with a bath in it and for an extra tuppence I could have the water brought up and bathe fully. Thankfully she did not ask about my fallen sister. I had to wait in the lodgers' parlour until it was ready and drifted off in the softest armchair until a rude voice snapped,

"Mr. Vail — it's ready," and one of the servant girls thrust her hand into my face, "Tuppence!"

The water eased all my aches, even my hips and lower back, and I allowed my muscles to soften and stretch out. My mind floated around Ina, the tree, the shed, her father and onions until the feeling that had been hiding stepped forward and woke me fully. Would McMahon and Walsh get to Ina before her father could stop them? I dried and dressed then as I could not walk the few steps to my room wrapped in the thin towel that was included with the tuppence. Once there, I dropped my dirty clothes on the floor and had to remind myself with relief that there was no longer a gun to hide, then I wriggled into my nightshirt and slid under the eiderdown for a short nap.

It was dark when I awoke from a dreamless sleep and looking at my fob watch without a candle was a challenge, but it seemed to be saying four o'clock and everything was silent apart from the noisy owl in the graveyard trees. I had slept for fourteen hours and hunger danced a jig in my stomach. There would be no food at that hour, so I lit the candle, took out my notebook and began to write down everything as it had happened up until then. Dawn came up slowly heralded by a loud choir of little birds and I dressed quickly hoping to be the first at breakfast.

Jim was there but I did not get the chance to question him further about my 'friend' as he left after a coughing fit, giving me his sausage and fried bread slice as he did. Two breakfasts and two hot teas later I left my laundry on the bed for the maid to collect and set off for the Chronicle, ready to face whatever transpired. On the way I passed the hole where the fountain had been and two urchins jumping in and out of the muddy puddle it had left. My intention was to drop into the barbers again, if there was no queue, and sort out my facial hair. Hopefully grooming my moustache back to its perfect shape would finish the picture I intended to portray of confidence and purpose.

Inside I soon got a chair and work began as I leaned back and closed my eyes. Another customer entered and chatted with the barber about the weather and the fountain's removal — apparently he was not happy as it had been designed for a competition by his cousin's son and the poor lad had drowned at sea before it was finished. The smell of soapy foam and Macassar oil floated around us as the sharp blade scraped away. It took a moment for the turn of the conversation to penetrate my relaxation and my sudden jump could have caused my death.

"So, they caught the Fenian leader then—the one with the explosives? What a low life eh?"

I opened my eyes and saw the barber's pale faced expression of shock. "For the love of God sir—keep still—I could scar you for life—or worse!"

I had to apologise profusely, then force myself to stay still as my heart beat fast and the feeling of comfort evaporated. The conversation moved on to the price of a good horse and gossip about the morals of lady performers in the music hall nearby and when I got down from the chair I was not sure which of the three waiting men was the one who had spoken. I did not want to admit my interest in Fenians to the shop at large. Five minutes later I entered the Chronicle building, anxiety twisting my stomach anew. I was determined to confront Nathaniel and the danger he had placed me in and to discover whether Mr. Maguire had been captured. Putting the loss of his nest behind him, Caligula strolled forward to greet me and a most welcome voice called,

"Come back at once or it will be trouble for you," followed by the rest of Maud holding a fish head in a napkin. She stopped abruptly when she saw me, "Thank goodness you are here! You can explain to them before Nathaniel blackens your name," nodding towards the office door, "Go on—they still think you are rescuing your sister."

I straightened my cravat in Queen Victoria's reflection and ruffled Caligula's ears before taking a deep breath and striding up to the door.

Inside, the room was disturbingly crowded and as I entered all the occupants seemed to speak at once. Mr. Creed's shout of 'Enough Gentlemen!' had the desired effect and I was able to sort out who they were.

Nathaniel stood beside the gun man and James Ward sat at Henry's desk. Behind him, hat in hand, stood Officer I'Anson from the tragedy in the market-place and Mr. Creed was at his own desk. There was no sign of Henry. The officer leant over Mr. Ward and spoke into his ear loudly enough for us all to hear, "Well here's a surprise! Should I arrest him now sir?"

I swallowed hard and resisted the very strong urge to run. "Arrest?" I managed to gasp.   Surveying them all it came to me that they had been discussing my crimes for some time. Nathaniel had a composed but serious look and the rest of them seemed like men who had come to a grave but sensible conclusion based on his evidence.

"Rescued your sister did you? Or were you actually on other business?" Nathaniel asked. Strangely, although I could be facing prison or even death I did not feel daunted, so I began.

"My sister did not need rescuing, Sirs. I have been involved in far greater matters for what seems like a lifetime and I must be allowed to explain in detail."

"Mr. Creed—" Nathaniel started to interrupt but Creed waved him down, "No Nathaniel—he has a right to speak and besides this could be entertaining!" He leaned back in his leather chair comfortably while Nathaniel muttered under his breath and fidgeted. So, I told them everything—or what I wanted them to believe was everything.

Silence pervaded the room when I finished speaking until the gun man, who had not been introduced, cleared his throat, "Thank you for that Mr. Vail—indeed the law thanks you too. You will be pleased to know that the Fenian leader has been arrested and is now languishing in Newcastle Gaol."

"What is his name? I was not told it when he locked me up," I improvised quickly.

"McMahon, I believe?" James Ward looked to the man who was clearly his boss for confirmation.

"Yes—it will be in the press later today anyway so is not a secret. So now I must apologise for all you have been through Mr. Vail. You and Mr. Parkes here have done us a service, even though you could not have specifically understood the mission you were on. It has turned out well. Fenian leaders in Esh Winning have been uncovered and the explosive plot foiled."

A cold feeling ran down my spine as I realised that if I had not returned, these agents were willing to allow me to take the blame for all of it.

"Indeed—this whole state of affairs irks me somewhat gentlemen. Young Vail here was put in a dangerous position by both you and Mr. Parkes. Perhaps you could explain yourself Nathaniel? Surely you could have taken the gun and hidden it without involving an innocent in the endeavour?" Mr. Creed asked.

At this, I'Anson spoke up, "Mr Parkes wouldn't want to be caught with a murder weapon now would he, Sir?"

We all looked at Nathaniel, who reddened then stuttered, "Well er—he would not be—he was more expendable—an easy dupe."

At that moment all the tension and anger that my time with a murderer's gun had built in me exploded and I leapt around the desks and grabbed his fancy cravat before Mr. Creed and I'Anson each caught an arm and pulled me away, denying me the satisfying blow I was about to deliver.

"No solution there, Thadeus!" Creed said, freeing me. "Mr. Ward, I assume that there is very little of this that I can publish without revealing all your undercover activities?"

"Precisely. No one at the Iron Works must know my true identity. Perhaps a story about the gun being found and the apprehension of McMahon, possibly embellished with one about the dangers of Fenianism, their despicable plot being foiled, and the rail line saved, but that is all." He picked up his hat from the table, nodded to I'Anson and made to rise and leave, "Oh, and Creed—here is your money back!" and threw a coin dismissively onto the desk.

They filed out, the gun man last, and as he went he nodded to me, "Time to pull the carrots up, eh?" I felt the strength leave me then and sank down onto my chair. They knew. There were even more layers to this than I had just witnessed.

Left alone, Mr. Creed cleared his throat. "I must say that I am shocked by your deception and your use of two innocents, Nathaniel— Thadeus and my niece Maud. I can see, however, that the police must have a system to undermine dangerous villains and that it can only work through secrecy. As for you, Mr. Vail, I thought you might have come to me sooner, particularly as you believed Maud to be in danger."

I thought of all the times I had made up my mind to do just that and had been stumped by some snag or another. Of course, I couldn't explain this to him by then as I had succeeded in hiding all I knew about Ina and her family's involvement with the Fenians.

"I'm sorry Sir but I was under pressure and in some danger. Nathaniel hid the truth from me too—I had trusted him." I was aware then that I sounded like my old timid self—Mother would have called me a whinger.

After that, it was agreed that Mr. Creed would not press further on the matter but demanded that we both vow to always appraise him of the truth. To my surprise, and not a little delight, he told Nathaniel that he had decided to send him to our sister farming paper in Barnard Castle to gain some experience as the Deputy Editor there and that he could start the following week. Nathaniel realised that arguing would be futile, and it would be a step towards improving his status on his return. So there was little more to be said.

Mr. Creed handed me an article to write up concerning complaints about dirty water in a well in one of the yards and sent Nathaniel out to report on the health benefits of the spa waters at Croft. I smiled to myself as he slammed the door behind him, cursing the cat loudly as he went. Henry entered passing him on the way in, with, "Well, someone's got their dander up! Come on—tell all — did you save your sister then?"

"Later, or we'll have no copy for tonight's edition!"

I sighed and shrugged at Henry, hoping that I had conveyed enough of a promise for later enlightenment, and dipped a nib in the ink well and began to write.

Chapter 14

Nathaniel did not speak to me again before he left even though I tried to confront him further. He made much of his 'promotion' to Henry but managed to never be alone with me.

The first evening I found myself in my room with little to do I took the opportunity to write to my parents with a good story about Etta. As far as they were to know she was safe and well and living somewhere in London with Bridie. They had no knowledge of her address and as I believed London to be a big place, hoped that might deter their search. I emphasised that she was not actually fallen and would return to them intact and ripe for the marriage market within a few weeks. Mother, I knew, would be happy to let her go for now in those circumstances, though Father did have a certain fondness for his wayward daughter.

I sat back, somewhat satisfied with the image I had created and just a little worried that what Etta said she felt for Tom was actually love. The thought of what they must be getting up to pulled my thoughts to Cornsay Colliery and the shape of Ina. Would she be safe now with Walsh still free? The gun man's hint as he left had sent a shiver through me as it seemed to show that the police knew all about the Maguire connection to the Fenian plot. I found myself standing at the window staring down into the late evening gloom in the graveyard behind the church, searching for a glimpse of her and imagining rushing down to meet her in the lane, throwing my arms around her to ease the ache in my body. Sometimes her absence was almost painful. I had to see her again but arriving at Cornsay without a clear purpose could mean that she would not be there, or perhaps her brothers or father would not allow me to see her at all.

Shaking myself out of my reverie I headed downstairs to place the letter on the table in the hall, ready to be taken to the post the next morning. Standing on the dark tiles I suddenly felt I could not just go back up to bed, and grabbing the large cap, which I had grown to rather like by then, from the hat stand, I left in search of entertainment. I found an inn which seemed busy with both the right and wrong sort of customers and entering the warm noisy tobacco fog, pushed my way to the bar.

"You going up?" asked the shirt sleeved barman.

"Where?"

"Upstairs to the entertainment!" He was having to shout to be heard. "Six pence entry then, Sir." He pointed to a busy set of stairs, handed me a tankard and held out a hand for payment in quick succession.

So, I found myself in what seemed to be a small theatre with tables for the audience and slid into a spare seat beside a man and woman who ignored me and continued kissing and touching each other in a most inappropriate way for a public space.

Music stuck up from somewhere and a young woman and much older man stepped forward. To my surprise they began a love scene from a play I had read. Two lovers—Romeo and Juliet—were vowing undying love in her chamber as the dawn came up and would force them to part. They put remarkable pathos into the whole thing, although one or two ribald audience members called out, 'Is he not yer Da, love?' and 'Watch out he doesn't drop on the job!' People generally stopped walking about and pursuing other activities until they had finished. After them, a singer entered and gave a moving rendition of 'Come into the garden, Maud', followed by a local song in a jargon I could not make out. He received applause and cheers. Finally, a short figure with long curled hair, a tankard in one hand and a stool in the other, came and sat at the front of the stage. All became silent as he placed his stool and sat on it. The audience obviously knew and anticipated his performance. As he started to speak, someone in the background began to play a fiddle softly.

"'Tis a tale of the great hero Fionn Macoul, his son, and a band of brave Fenian knights."

A murmur ran through the audience but no one called out or interrupted. I found myself leaning forward to listen, for he did not shout like the actors had done and was lost in the tale of battles, giants, mysterious powers and the gift of foretelling the future through the chewing of a thumb. Even though the idea to a rational mind was quite preposterous, I felt wrapped in a magical coat of some kind when he finished, and, not wanting to lose its enchantment, I pushed my way out through the applause and headed home.

It was on the way that the plan came to me. The tale had reminded me of Ina and her father; I could put it to Mr. Creed that I should go and interview him and put together stories of his journey to England in instalments, as people liked them so well. The bonus for me of course would be to see Ina every week. My steps hurried on and if I had known where he lived, I would have knocked on Mr. Creed's door immediately with such a fine idea.

The next morning when I arrived, the Chronicle was in a fever. The following week was to be the fiftieth anniversary of the start of the railways and, as their birthplace, the town was organising great celebrations. Henry and I were sent out together to interview locals involved in this and gather information on the plan of the day, which was to be a holiday for all. Mr. Creed was going to speak with the architect of the huge statue which was to be placed to honour a local dignitary, Joseph Pease, who had become known as the 'father of the railways'. Amidst all the excitement I did manage to put my idea to Creed but he merely said he would consider it later. There was to be a special edition of the paper on the day, which would be a Monday, so we had to work all week with no Sunday off.

For three days, Henry and I had gone out visiting different areas which were beginning their preparations and talked to as many people as we could, to get their stories. The Sunday broke warm and sunny for late September and we agreed to separate and take in the places where the main festivities were being planned.

The town were organising a grand parade, an evening banquet, exhibitions of locomotives and the grand statue unveiling amongst a general atmosphere of a fair day with roast meat to buy and ale aplenty. Outside the offices, the marketplace was receiving cart loads of fresh flowers to hang from the columns, which men were working on with much hammering and shouting. White, pink and yellow roses were to form chains from pillar to pillar and beyond them, barrels of ale were being rolled from carts down into gaping cellar doors ready to slake the thirst of more customers at one time than most of the publicans had ever seen. Most people I spoke to seemed brimming with excitement and focussed with purpose on their tasks — though a few men on a bench sampling the first of the ale were dismissive of the rule of the Pease family because of their teetotal ways and dislike of the music halls. The statue's subject had been a mine owner as well as a railway man and they expressed sympathy with workers who held his substantial wealth, which was based on their own safety and lives, to be a detriment to his memory. Mulling this over, I left the market place and made my way to the graveyard where an elderly lady had told me he was buried.

Instead of the garden in front of the big church where Ina and I had stopped, it was a little square behind a building, near to where the music hall tent had been on the night Henry and I visited. Rows of perfectly even grey stones stood beside each other, none larger or more ornate than its neighbour.

A man all in black walked slowly up and down between them. He didn't seem to see me at first and as I looked, I found there were many bearing the name Pease, so I approached him to ask the whereabouts of Joseph.

"Are you a friend?" was his reply.

Puzzled, I thought that as I was not his enemy then I must be, "Yes Sir. I hope so."

At that he smiled, "Ah! I see you are not then. Here—you stand beside his stone."

After a glance to verify the name, I felt somewhat embarrassed and attempted to converse again. "It is peaceful here, is it not?"

"He wanted peace, alive and dead, it was his belief."

"You knew him then? What were his beliefs?" I knew my father would pronounce on sin and punishment, obedience to laws and the rightness of his views if asked that question.

"Integrity, simplicity, equality, community and peace should just about cover it I would say."

"But why are there no tombstones, no weeping angels, no shiny blocks of marble to honour the dead?"

"Well—I told you why already, young man. Simplicity and equality."

"But—" I began to ask the question we were both thinking of at the same moment he answered it, "Sometimes the community wants to show their gratitude with a memorial, but here is where he truly lies beneath the green grass and brown earth." At this he turned to follow the path out of the place in the direction of the building which fronted the graveyard and I realised I had not asked his name. He was a sprightly mover and I just caught up with him at the door. I asked my question but was not sure I had heard the answer correctly as, without turning, he replied, "Joseph—Joseph Pease."

A little shaken at the thought that I may have encountered the statue's ghostly embodiment, and vowing to tell Henry about this, I noticed that clouds were beginning to gather and the day became a little chill. Setting off down the busy hill towards the cricket ground where we had agreed to meet I saw him underneath an eye catching archway bearing the legend 'Pioneers of Railway Enterprise'. It was decorated with even more roses and through it could be seen a huge tent which covered a long table yet to be laid for the next day's banquet. He was deep in conversation with Maud Lemon.

"How beautiful is all this?" I called to them and consigned the strange encounter in the graveyard to the back of my mind. Maud's uncle had allowed her to come out with us and interview people, as he sometimes did when he thought it suitable.

"I wish I could be here tomorrow evening,' she smiled, "Mayors, dignitaries, important people, even members of parliament filling up the table!"

"And their interminably boring speeches!" reminded Henry, "Come on, let's get something to eat in the market, and an ale or two while we're there."

Later, feeling a little fatigued, we sat at our desks and reported as much as we could of what we had seen and heard. Maud wrote hers at the reception desk, Caligula curled around her feet. There was no sign of Mr. Creed, although when he did return later he seemed a little unsteady on his feet.

That night whirled itself into a crashing storm. Behind the house, the graveyard yews waved and bent themselves in a manic dance and the window shook and rattled in its wooden frame. I dreamed of Will again floating up from the yard on a gust, his polished buttons clattering against the glass and his voice calling in an echo, 'Do not go—not go—not go', then a long drawn out 'Thadeus', which finally jerked me awake. I kept the counterpane over my head and listened until I could convince myself it was just the wind, and fall asleep again.

Next day it was raining hard and I wondered if the tent in the cricket field still stood. After breakfast I made my way down through the main streets, noticing the absence of geese or any other livestock as I fell in with a growing crowd of wetly hurrying people. I had agreed to meet Henry near the statue and see if we could get a glimpse under its cover. It was quite easy at that early hour and despite the rain getting heavier we managed to view the black panels that surrounded its pedestal displaying images of freed slaves, locomotive engine, children at school and what seemed like officials of some sort, before we were sent on our way by a couple of soldiers who should have been guarding it better. After that, we made our way to see the exhibition of engines at North Road then managed to squeeze onto the special train back to the station where I had first arrived in Darlington.

There we tagged along beside the Grand Procession and arrived back in the town centre to wait for the unveiling with a sausage and a lump of bread each from a stall. The clouds cleared by midday and we staked a place near to the high wooden podium which had been built for the speeches to come. There was much jollity abroad and we were entertained by a barrel organ player and his dancing monkey, several singers looking to fill their hats with coins, and even a not very handy juggler. Thankfully this passed the time as it was not until five o'clock that the statue was to be unveiled.

At least the rain had stopped earlier but we were both soaked and I felt I would never dry out. Several speeches began in praise of railway, industry and learning, as well as the man himself and I began to notice my leg and hip aching as I tried to hear them. Just when it seemed to be never ending, a group of young soldiers with bugles pushed their way through, and all was finally ready to pull the cord and reveal the statue to the world. A man had stepped forward and to my dismay began another speech, the cord wrapped around his hand. He was all in black and I began to realise I had seen him before.

"Who is that?" I asked Henry who was slightly closer than me.

"It's—I think it's—yes I can make him out now — Joseph Pease!"

"But isn't he dead—not unveiling his own statue?"

"Eh? It's his son—he has a W before the Pease I believe! How could it be him, you wooden spoon?"

Somehow it seemed the Member of Parliament looked right at me as he spoke. The nine foot high figure with his hand in his jacket looked blankly down on all of us as the trumpeters blasted out, and the day for most of us came to an end.

"Let's go to the King's Head and get a meal and a drink," Henry suggested— and with hindsight I became a wooden spoon again.

It seemed very hot inside the busy bar and three flagons did not satisfy my thirst. I knew I had to leave and perhaps cool down on the walk back to my lodgings although I could not understand the shivering that overtook me. Henry had gone on with some friends who had been in the inn and I was alone with pains shooting through both my legs and up my back and a feeling that the sausage I had eaten earlier was making its way back to the daylight. I remember almost dragging myself up the stairs at Linden House, then nothing more.

Apparently I had slept for two days before anyone went to check whether I still lived, and I came to, coughing furiously into Maud's face. Sleep was what I desired most and I do recall wondering how Maud could tell Mr. Creed about her improper behaviour in entering a gentleman's bedroom, then drifting off again. Mrs. Furness felt that applying a hot poultice would cure my cough and in the first week I woke up to what seemed like a burning chest and the smell of linseed and mustard.

Gradually I began to spend a little more time awake and Henry brought me laudanum drops in warm milk, which certainly cheered my soul if nothing else and allowed my chest muscles, aching from coughing, to relax a little. Many dreams came with them, mostly quite happy ones, and some beautiful, as Ina's naked form climbed into bed with me and her hands moved gently across my body.

When I finally returned to life, the doctor that Mrs. Furness had called decreed that I no longer needed laudanum and I could begin to try some time back at work. So, it was late October when I finally left the house feeling rung out but determined to get to the real Ina again.

Chapter 15

I had written to Ina with my proposition before I had got permission from Mr. Creed and there was a letter waiting for me on the post table in the hall when I descended on slightly shaky legs that first morning. I did not recognise the hand so I assumed it must be hers and opened it carefully.

She told me that she had persuaded her father, with little effort it seemed, to agree to my writing of his journey and life so far as long as I did not write about the Fenians. He owed them some secrecy having taken an oath to that effect. The letter gave no hint at affection and I had no idea whether it had cooled after such an absence, but the excitement of seeing her again was enough for me. It was a Friday and with the help of her letter Mr. Creed agreed to my plan as long as I used Sundays for the interviews, which was the day that Mr. Maguire would be free to sit and talk.

The days were shorter, dark and cold and the air bit. I silently thanked Bridie for my big overcoat as I stepped off the train at Cornsay Colliery. The early drawing in of evening outlined the huge dark shape of the colliery against a starless sky. My bag bulged with tobacco for Mr. and Mrs Maguire, almond comfits for the rest of the family and pink sugar plums for Kieran. Although I would have loved to give Ina her own gift, I had been taught that it was not appropriate for a young man to give gifts to any woman who was not his fiancé. I drew a long breath and set off down the nesting row of squat buildings, rehearsing in my head the best way to approach Michan Maguire. Deep in thought, I was unprepared for the figure which appeared from an alley and threw themselves upon me. In shock, I unpeeled the arms which wrapped around me and prepared to attempt to talk myself out of any danger, when a familiar chuckle added to the voice I had been aching to hear,

"Thadeus—it's me! No need to fight! I am no púca!" She removed her shawl then and kissed me. I confess at that moment I would have left the story of her father and found a place to be alone again, but she broke off first and took my hand to lead me to her house.   "Da's story first I think!"

Moments later I sat at the big table, warmed by the stove and the proximity of several members of the Maguire family, wrapped in the tobacco fug from Mary and Michan's pipes. Thomas and Sean were out, much to my relief, but Aisling and her husband Kevin were there and to my embarrassment, though no one else's, she openly undid her bodice to nurse the latest baby whenever it stirred. Kieran and his niece Eliza played on the floor together with a tin of wooden buttons.

So, we began. I explained to the company that I wanted to write about Michan and Mary's journeys from Ireland and although I would like to hear everything, I knew that some elements of the recent past could not be written.

"Aye, no Fenian talk mind," affirmed Mary. Michan leaned back taking a pull on his pipe and began. His voice became a soothing trail through a time of horror. I knew as

I wrote that people would be interested to read it—so many like me ignorant of those events of over twenty years past. There were still many even then who would choose not to believe his words and continue to hold on to the image of the ignorant Irish monkey, drowned in drink and unable or unwilling to help himself. We are led to believe that honest labour will save us, and I still hold to this in some measure—and that there is a place for us all to live well, as long as we keep to our station. Any other way leads us to poverty, hunger and death through our own fault. However, it will be forever hard to shake the picture—now it has been planted in my head—of a child carrying the body of his dead sister down to the graveyard and throwing earth and leaves over her, hoping that animals who are starving too do not find it.

Michan stopped when he arrived at his meeting with his boy's namesake, Kieran, just after his brave but unsuccessful attempt to save the lad's father—and gave way to Mary. Her journey had been similar but her family had left the country together before the brown mist of the blight spread across the potato rows and her father went to work down the mine with his cousins soon after they arrived.

Aisling, who had been much affected by hearing the story fully for the first time asked, "Tell us one of your tales now, Da—one that is not so sad. We need cheering before we take the bairns home." Kieran climbed onto Michan's knee as he began.

"One evening about this time of year when the spirits have most power over all things, a pretty girl had gone to the well for water. Her foot slipped and she fell and when she got up and looked around it seemed to her as if she were in a strange place as all around had changed as if by enchantment. In the distance she saw a great crowd gathered around a glowing fire and she felt drawn towards them, but even when they surrounded her they did not speak and when she tried to turn and leave them she could not move. Then a beautiful youth with a red sash and long flowing yellow hair came up and asked her to dance with him. She refused as there was no music playing but he made a sign to the silent people and suddenly the sweetest music flowed around and over her and they danced and danced until the moon and stars went down. She forgot everything in the world except the dance, the beautiful music and her partner. After they finished, they asked her to feast with them and led her down a flight of steps to a large hall all bright and shining with gold and silver lights and a table groaning with good things to eat and drink. But as she was about to drink someone passed close to her and whispered, 'Eat no food and drink no wine or you will never see your home again'.

Suddenly the strange people were all angry calling, 'Whoever comes to us must eat and drink with us'. But the whispering man took her arm and led her out just in time. 'You are safe for now', he told her. 'Take this herb and hold it in your hand until you reach home'. And he gave her a branch of Athair-Luss, which we know as ground ivy. This she took and fled along the dark sward, all the while hearing voices behind her. 'You are safe now but when you dance again to the music on the hill, you will stay with us forever more, and none shall hinder', they called. But she kept the magic branch safe and the Sidhe never troubled her more. It was long and long before the sound of the fairy music left her ears or the memory of her fairy suitor on that dark November night."

Kieran yawned and little Eliza was asleep on Kevin's knee. "I think the fairies have taken this one, Da" he said, "Thanks for such a tale. It is a long while since I have heard ones like that myself." We all made to rise and the adults began to move the chairs and table and prepare the room to become a bedroom. I offered to help, my head full of fairy music but Ina said she would see me out and I took the chance of a few moments alone with her. Outside the front door the night had grown brighter with a rising moon and we stood close, enjoying the crisp cool after the too warm kitchen.

"Thank you for the sweetmeats, Thadeus, and for getting Da to begin his tale. He has kept much of that from us 'til now. It was very sad—I see now why he kept it to himself." I tried to put my arms around her at this, but she pulled away.

"I can see I may need some ground ivy for you! There will be talk and questions if we are seen. Next Sunday, come early and we can walk out on the fell—you never know I might slip and fall, then find a beautiful prince to ask me to dance!" I left, full of hope for her invitation and the article I was about to write.

Next morning life seemed to have stabilised itself into the form I had been expecting before I arrived and was handed that gun. Mr. Creed was impressed that I had already got some good copy from the Maguires and we agreed to run it the following Friday. I felt some disappointment that I had not been able to add to the reporting on the railway anniversary celebrations, but Maud was very pleased to have taken my place and even get her name on one of the pieces that she,

Henry and Mr. Creed had put together. At the morning meeting I was sent to speak to the head of the Training College for Elementary School Mistresses about the excitement of moving to a much more modern building which was one of the many going up not far from my lodgings at Linden House. There was to be a large garden where the young ladies could exercise; filling my imagination with images of flushed young women at this task I left, intending to accept her invitation to return the following week and witness it personally.

Back in the market I was gratified at gaining a nod from the pie seller and what sounded like, 'Y'all right?' The small bubble of contentment that gave me was the first time that I acknowledged to myself that I was actually settling in and beginning to enjoy my job, even without the thrill of Fenian plots.

Maud was at her place in the entrance hall feeding Caligula dubious looking shiny white globules of animal innards and we chatted for a while as I ate my pie taking care not to look inside it. In a while, Henry swept in hatless, clean shaven and floppy haired and handed me a letter with a mock bow to Maud as he did.

"Ooh! More from the fallen woman?" he jibed as he tried to lean over my shoulder and watch me open it. I could see it was from Etta by her hand so I pushed him away, took up my hat and went into the office to read it in peace. His low and Maud's higher tones floated through the closed door as I sat down at my desk.

2, Hunt Street
Notting Hill

London

My dearest Thadeus

I am still safe and well and enjoying all that London has to offer. Tom and I stay with Bridget and her sister Kathleen, her husband Poraic and Cathal, their son. They run a general store and we live above this in comfort. More than anything I would love you to pay us a visit but this letter is also to ask you a favour of sorts. Mother and Father will be alone this Christmas season so their thoughts may turn again to finding me. Could you please, please, please Thadeus, find it in your heart to visit them for a few days and distract their interest? Our address is at the top of the letter in case you have mislaid it. As before, please Do Not Reveal it to them .Thank you! Thank You!

Your loving sister
Etta

I folded it slowly and pushed it back into the envelope. It was so like Etta to ask a favour then just accept that I would comply all in the same letter. When I asked Mr. Creed later about holidays at Christmas he was insistent that with all I had been through I should have a few days to visit Prickwillow—in reality this time—and would hear no argument against the enterprise.

With a mixture of feelings, I would have to accept that there was no way to avoid the trip but for the time remaining I looked forward to at least another three Sundays with Ina and the promise of walking out together on the fell.

Chapter 16

It turned out to be our only chance to be alone before Christmas as soon after the weather grew biting teeth, dressing the bare trees in white lace and hardening the glassy ground with slides of ice.

That day though, when we met at the station in the late morning, a weak sun still kept a little warmth in the November air. Ina's eyes sparkled from under a heavier shawl and she wore a long coat that looked like it could have been Thomas or Sean's, giving her a fairy look. We both carried a bag with simple food and wore sturdy boots. I had pushed a copy of the Chronicle in too, in order to show the family later.

"It was a rush to get through Mass and breakfast to get here! Ma thinks I have gone off to visit old Martha who lives with her brother Jim's family in Esh Winning. I should be safe from discovery—Martha's thoughts are not tied down—she will never remember if I came or not!"

It took us under an hour to leave the smoke of industry behind and step out into the clearer air. Away from spying eyes, we could link arms and stop to kiss when the feeling took us. Although so much has changed since that day, I always keep the sweetness of it stowed away in my thoughts.

Shelters for sheep leaned here and there against a long

wall fitted together with many shaped dry stones, and as there were no sheep around we chose one of the small huts to spread Ina's shawl in and sit and eat. There was dry straw at its base and a strong smell of lanolin.

"Well, it is little worse than you in the allotment shed!" she teased.

Feigning indignation, I turned away but she prodded me in the back, "I am prepared to overlook it this time I suppose, Thadeus!" Her voicing my name always undid me and when I turned back her hands pulled me down wrapping me in her open coat.

"I will wash for you next time—I promise", and I stretched out, fitting myself into the curves of her body until we could not hold back and helped each other clumsily remove some of our suddenly constricting garments. We only lay a little while afterwards as the air had become colder and there did not seem to be much to be said. Later, on the way back we found our voices and talked of sharing a house together and laying in a warm feather wrapped bed —though we both stopped short of imagining a marriage. I knew even then I could not see myself living in a house such as hers, going down into the dangerous dark every day, and I wondered how lost she would feel in my world. Just before we reached the village in the early dusk she stood on tiptoe for a last kiss, then pulled away and sighed,   "Where is the man from the story to whisper in my ear and save me, love?" A shock ran through me then as she had called me love.

"You are safe without him Ina—I do not live in a rath underground and you have only eaten your own food!"

We both laughed and shook the Sidhe off. "I'm going to

find some ground ivy now though," she said, "Before we get to Ma and Da smelling of sheep!"

Even more family members were there when we arrived. Aisling and Ina's sister Peig and both their husbands sat around the table adding to the tobacco clouds with their pipes and a young woman very like Ina who introduced herself as Maggie, their cousin. We tried to look as innocent as possible when Maggie asked, "Did you meet at the station then? That was luck with you coming from Esh Winning Ina, and him from Durham!"

Ina took her place beside Mary and smiled around the table, "Aye—tis lucky I am indeed Maggie—with me taking the path round by the station and bumping into this one." She seemed about to question us further but Michan spoke up, "You're welcome Mr. Vail—come take this chair by me and we can begin. The cold air has made you flushed and I know you have been ill not long since." He looked directly at me as he spoke and for a moment I was sure he knew quite well where we had been and what we had been doing. I handed him the paper, open at the article, as I sat but he pushed it to one side, "For later."

His story that time took us to when he had stowed away on a canal boat and gave us magical pictures of flying high over tall aqueducts, skimming frozen tree-tops and sleeping on prickly flax stalks. All in the room held their breath when he described the boat sinking down through wet walls and exclaimed in relief when they discovered, like him, that it was a lock. Aisling led the call for one of his tales after that and as everyone joined her with enthusiasm, he agreed to begin another.

"There were many festivals and feasts the mortals kept in the good years of Eire but at those times the fairies were not idle either. At times when the mortals were at their happiest Finvarra the King and his chosen band were on the watch to carry off the prettiest girls to the fairy mansions. There they kept them for seven years and at the end of that time, when they grew old and ugly, they were sent back— for fairies love nothing so much as youth and beauty. As a compensation for this slight put upon them, those women were taught all the fairy secrets and the magic that lies in herbs as well as the strange power they have over disease. So, by this means, the women became all powerful with their charms, spells and potions and could kill or save as they chose.

Now, there was a woman of the islands greatly feared because of this power. She collected herbs to use secretly and alone for no one must see or touch them or they would lose their power. She was known as the fairy doctress. Now, one time a mortal man came to her for help for he was lame from a fall and could do no work. The doctress had the power of divination from the fairies too and when she knew that he was coming she prepared a potion from herbs and salves to cure him. He told her that one time he had been in the mountains and slipped and fell on his face and when he rose up his leg was powerless though no bones were broken. She told him that she knew how it had happened as he had trodden on a herb under which fairies were resting. This so angered them that they struck him on the leg and lamed him. 'But my power is greater than theirs. Do as I say and you will soon be cured', she said. He took the salve and potion she gave him and used it in silence and alone as she had instructed, and in three days the power came back to his leg. He was so grateful he offered her silver but she said, 'I do not sell knowledge, I give it. In this way the strength and power remain with me forever'."

In the silence that followed I managed to calm my mind but I knew that Michan was talking of me in the story and the doctress must be Ina in some way. I thanked him and Mary and gathered up my notebook and pencils rather clumsily. The spell broken, much chatter ensued as the family set to moving the furniture and changing the room to its night time character again. A tug on my arm was Ina leading me to the front door, past little Kieran already asleep in his wooden cradle. No one looked at the newspaper or commented upon it. Outside I could hold it no longer. "He knows Ina—he knows we did not meet at the station—I think he was warning me!"

"Oh, I know he was! But my strength and power remain with me—I will protect you, cara! And don't worry about the paper—I will read it to him later."

On the train back to Darlington the thought came to me again—however much we wanted it, was our enjoyment in each other dishonest? I could hear Mother's voice in the background somewhere talking to Will before he left for the army, 'Lower class girls have no morals. You may have your pleasure if you must—then you leave!' I shut her image down and allowed myself to replace it with one of Ina next Sunday. She had called me 'love' for the first time and that was all that mattered.

As it transpired, we only had one more week as the miners were expected to work the Sunday before Christmas Eve in order to have a holiday on that day, returning to work on the evening of the following day. We had made no arrangement to meet earlier again and in any case an icy rain drenched everything the whole day. The same people were in the Maguire's dwelling when I arrived and no one had come to meet the train. I had more almond comfits and sugar plums as a Christmas Eve gift and tobacco for their pipes. Michan stood warming his backside against the fire in the range and Kevin played with the children on the floor, his infant son cradled on his outstretched legs as Kieran and Eliza rolled a wooden ball back and forth.

"Sit yerself down lad." Mary nodded to me and a cold memory of McMahon and Walsh's interrogation in the hut floated into my mind. But Ina broke the moment with, "If yer bum's toasted enough now, Da, you could sit too!"

Whatever I had thought was going to happen, didn't. Everyone picked handfuls of comfits and sugar plums, filling the room with crunching and sucking sounds of appreciation. Michan picked up last week's paper and placed it with the new one in front of him. "Thank you for these. Tis strange to see yourself from outside eyes like this but you told it well!"

That time he took us all to Belfast to an alley by the port where he had so bravely fought two robbers, but still lost everything. At that point, he stopped to fill his pipe and cough heavily. Everyone chatted while he did this and got his breath back with a few long sucks, then Peig cut through it all, "We must have a tale now, Da, if you're well enough. Can you tell us the one about The Demon Cat?" Of course, though the stories were new to me, Michan and Mary's children would have known them from being as small as Eliza and Kieran.

When he had finished—he never coughed when recounting a tale— he leaned back," 'Tis thanks from all of my beautiful family here, for the tales in the newspaper and my own story too. They need to be told—all of them—and written." Standing up a little clumsily he reached out and grasped my hand, "Visit your own for Christmas and come back to us in the January cold. We will be here." I noticed a slight nod towards Ina as he said it. So, he did know. Ina walked all the way back to the station with me and we took a detour down an alley to kiss and touch as much as we could in the icy rain.

Two weeks later, on the train down to Peterborough, I allowed the echo of that touch to fill my senses. It banished the images of dead Will and the grey emptiness of long Prickwillow days. I knew I was stronger by then but had no inkling of what was to come next.

Chapter 17

On the branch line to Ely I was struck by the clean lines of the endless flat landscape. No mines or smoke belching chimneys squat on the horizon to mar the view, although it still seeped into the cabin from the engine through the cracks where the carriage windows shut.   Consoling myself with the knowledge that I would only be with Father and Mother for a short while, the thought of how to cut it even shorter came to me. I would go down to London and find Etta and her new family. It would need to be secret, but I could kill two birds with one stone and still keep her safe from rescue and incarceration in the vicarage.

Much cheered by this, I found Ben waiting on the platform looking the same as when I left—which was a surprise as so much life had passed me by then it was hard to remember that it had in fact only been a few months. A man of few words, he told me only the basic information that my parents were well and that everyone missed Etta and Bridie, but no one knew their whereabouts. If he had been hiding any other knowledge it would have been difficult to tell. Before I knew it, the chase was pulling up at the gate and the vicarage's grey stone loomed in front of me. No one came to the door and I had to knock and wait. It was Father who eventually arrived, calling a rebuke over his shoulder to some maid who he considered lazy.

His look shocked me. Unlike Ben, the months had taken a toll upon him—his hair almost white and skin wrinkled into frown lines.

"Thadeus! We thought you would arrive later. Come in—come in. I am writing the sermon for Christmas Eve and Mother is resting."

"Is she well?" I asked dutifully as I entered.

"Tolerably so. She wishes to make her usual visit to Ely tomorrow and visit the grave before attending their Christmas Eve service. Go on up—your room is aired and ready."

He had glanced down on the word 'grave', still moved I supposed by its occupant, my twin Thomas, who had never lived. The name of William Edward was engraved upon it too, though of course he lay somewhere in that hot place thousands of miles away. There were no graves in Prickwillow of course as the occupants would float in the sodden ground and perhaps make their way down to the Lark. I had wanted to mention Etta then but thought the better of it at that moment, assuming it would come up later. My room—the old nursery—had a fire crackling in the grate and a still hot warming pan between the sheets. I pulled the old armchair up to the window and sat a while, gazing down the path which Will's ghost trod in my dreams. The land was slowly sinking beneath the building and there was one more front step to it since I had left. The accident came back to me then. Chasing Will up the tree in the bishop's garden in Ely, desperate as always to try and catch him up—the feel of my fingers slipping as I hung there, the adults shouting my name as if to save me with the sound. Then that amazing feeling of flying which had seemed to go on forever until I hit the blackness. After that, I became another person. The Thadeus confined to bed. No joining Will at school, a whole year trapped in bed and endless pain filled days until I was allowed to master my limp—my leg broken in two places, one remaining shorter than the other forever.

As I sat there, I felt almost as purposeless as I had then without an article to chase up and a print deadline to work to. Out on the river the sound of the steam side engine measured the minutes as heart beats, holding the waters back. I must have dozed off as the next thing I remember is the dinner bell clattering in the hall and I hurriedly changed and descended, passing the new maid who was lighting the gas lamps in the opposite direction. The dining room was a revelation. A tree stood in the corner draped with ribbons and hanging shapes of biscuits, marzipan and small colourful gift boxes. Even some of Will's old tin soldiers hung amidst the white candles dotted about its branches giving the whole thing a glittering quality.

My open mouth prompted Father to speak up. "It looks well does it not? It is that old tradition from Prince Albert's Germany—our new maid begged for it and for the first time Mother did not forbid it. Come take your seat, Thadeus. I hear her descending now."

My mind went from wonder to resentment with each approaching step. All those Christmases of cold sameness. Three children allowed down only for dinner—no decoration or concession of any sort, then back to the nursery with our Christmas tokens—a handkerchief, a comb, ribbons for Etta and one year, a set of drawing pencils which we all shared. I thought of Ina's family with perhaps similar gifts but also the warmth of being together, sharing Michan's tales and the binding company of love.

The door opened and Mother entered. She had also aged, her pinched face seeming more so if that were possible, the hair beneath her crocheted cap fully grey. Father and I stood for her to be seated then followed and looked at each other. Once the food came there would be no conversation allowed so I broke the silence first.

"Hello Mother. How charming it looks in here with that pretty tree—what allowed you to break with tradition this year?"

I heard Father suck in a surprised breath to my right but continued anyway.

"It was something our childhood lacked, was it not?"

"You are home, Thadeus—please have some respect. We want none of your worldly ways here."

"But surely such a tree is a worldly decoration, Mother?" I felt I could not stop at that point.

Father stepped in to diffuse the situation which I was building. "It is a sop to Molly, the new maid. She made all the decorations from her own pocket and there is also the old family bible upon that side table to remind us of the true meaning of the feast." He managed to admonish both of us in one sentence and sighed with relief as the food arrived. When all was finished we retired to the parlour together where the fire was bigger and all three of us shared a port.

"So, Molly is a good replacement for Bridie?" I opened with, sinking back into the deep plush of an armchair. The parlour was without any decoration and just as it had always been. Long heavy velvet curtains were drawn across the window and the four chairs still surrounded the hearth. They both spoke together,

"Nothing can......." from Father and

"She betrayed us, Thadeus," from Mother, "and took your sister from us. She is well lost to us. Such things are not forgivable."

"But is that not the true Christian way? To forgive!" Part of me could not recognise the Thadeus I had become but I was actually enjoying myself by then. Mother spluttered on her port.

"Etta is rendered useless now is she not? Whatever she has been doing there will always be a taint to her. We could not use her in a favourable marriage now even should she return home."

Putting thoughts of any possibility of an approving reaction to Ina aside, I continued, "You have one son left though," and waited for the sting.

She leaned forward, "You are barely capable of marriage with that damaged leg and such a disreputable choice of career. No, I am a childless mother now in every respect." Once again she had bested me and I lost control, jumping to my feet and toppling the port glass all over my trousers.

"Enough! You can discount me, but your daughter lives too. Go tomorrow and shed your pointless tears in Ely over the grave of the ones who can never disappoint you, but tell them too that Etta and I live and we *can* see the wide open world while yours festers here. Do not worry. I will be gone by St Stephen's day, just like her. Goodnight Mother—I leave you to your mourning weeds." My sweep out of the room was somewhat spoiled by Molly opening the door from the other side and unbalancing me.

Back up in the nursery I paced up and down, anger propelling me until, exhausted, I fell fully clothed onto my bed. Will's childhood one was still there on the other side of the room and Etta's through the door that led to Bridie's room. After a while my heart stopped pounding and I had just decided to undress and slide under the sheets when a gentle tapping sound came at the door. I had no thought it would be Mother but I did not want a lecture from Father either. However, the door opened and he stepped inside, not feeling any need for me to ask him in.

"Thadeus, can we speak in peace?"

I sighed, "Well, come right in then," then I sat upon the bed as he sank into the chair by the window. He held two more glasses of port and handed one to me.

"Now—whilst I cannot condone your rudeness towards your mother, I would ask you to grant a little leeway in your anger."

I interrupted him with a scornful grunt. "Why should she care what I say, rude or not? I am nothing to her, as she makes clear."

He leaned back and seemed to slip into some sort of reverie.

"When I met Anna she was just seventeen. Youngest daughter of a family with money and aristocratic pretensions. Her eyes sparkled and she lived for fun, constantly amusing me with her antics. My family loved her too and even though I was already twenty seven and still a curate, the match seemed perfect on both sides."

"That seems doubtful!" I muttered, but I do not think he heard.

"For a while we were so happy you know—but then the tragedies began. Her parents and sister drowned in a boating accident at sea off the coast, and just at the moment she had become pregnant for the first time. The baby came too soon—as they often do of course—but to lose three in a row is a hard tragedy for a young woman."

"But I did not—" I began.

"No, we have never spoken of it. For a while she would not come near me—you understand—but eventually we got Will and she was restored a little although something was missing which never came back to her. The sparkle I suppose. And the bitterness crept in in its place. Bridie had left us for a while but came back after Will was born and took over raising you all. Thomas was alive but only stayed with us a day. Twins take a lot of bearing and she was out of it for that time. She knew he had been alive and blamed me and Bridie for his death—and you I suppose."

A shock ran through me, "Me—but how?"

"She believes you took his life force by thriving."

My head was spinning. "Well, she always favoured Will but what about Etta?"

"She is dead to us now—and Will is truly dead. It is too late to turn Anna back but I will always try my best—for you. Please be kind to her while you are here—you will soon be gone."

He stood to end the talk then. As he left I wanted to

call him back and tell him I was going to find Etta, but the moment had passed.

Next day, Christmas Eve, I went to Ely with Mother to the grave and felt the dawning of a forgiveness towards her which was soon dissipated by her refusal to walk in with me and visit the seasonal market before the service in the abbey. Dinner that evening was not jolly, but a much calmer affair. Father allowed Molly and the new cook Mrs. Reed in to listen to him play carols on the parlour organ and sing along to them. All but Mother joined in heartily, but she did stay and watch. Afterwards, he gave them a lace edged handkerchief each and once they had cleared and washed all the dishes they could go home for a few hours until the midnight service. Of course, they would return the next day to prepare our Christmas feast. I noticed but did not make much of it at the time, that Molly gave all her smiles to Father.

The church was decorated with swathes of greenery and candles warmed it with a yellow glow as the villagers sang the old songs and tried to stay awake—greeting each other and Father heartily as they left. Dawn broke with rosy chill the next day, the sky stretching unhindered across the flat landscape of the fens. I gave Mother a comb and an embroidered notebook and Father a warm muffler and slippers made of felt. He gave me a muffler too and a fine pen with the emblem of Ely on it. We ate roast beef and goose and too much pudding, but Mother was at least civil. I did try to see her in the light Father had revealed to me, but a nagging doubt kept creeping in that surely all women were subject at times to such tragedies as hers but were able to put them away in their minds for the sake of the rest of their children. Mrs. Reed and

Molly had left us a cold spread of meat, goose, pickles, cheese and bread for the evening and gone off to join their own families.

So full I could hardly ascend the stairs I fell into bed and swiftly slept, though woke again in the dark from cheese dreams of Ina wading through a soggy graveyard to reach little Thomas who was swimming lifelike between the stones. Somehow I had to rescue her before she got to him but Will was shouting something to me from behind and a great fear of turning and seeing him overcame me as I woke repeating, 'You're dead, you're dead!' over and over. The room was cold without a fire and I could not find a flint to light the candle. It seemed forever until St Stephen's day brightened the window and I could rise and pack my valise.

Chapter 18

Our goodbyes that morning were perfunctory but at least Mother had come down and stood in the doorway to watch me go.

"Come back when you can," Father said, handing the valise up to the chase, then moved back to stand with Molly and they waved until we were out of sight.

The air was crisp and fresh and the short journey into Ely raised my spirits with every yard put between me and them. Leaving Ben with a tip for his troubles I boarded the train to Cambridge and then on to London. As far as anyone in Prickwillow knew, I was heading to Peterborough then home to the north east.

London hit my every sense as I walked out of Kings Cross Station. The noise of many voices selling their wares from stalls and trays hung about their necks competed with people rushing by me as if late for an important appointment. The smell of horse dung mixed with roasted meat, spices and fresh bread. Although it had been a bright day, smoke from the engines and tall fingered chimneys all around thickened the air, gas lamps fighting to penetrate it all. For a few moments I lost direction but then managed to find my way to a row of vehicles, their horses munching nosebags as they made a calm oasis in the general bustle. Assuming they must be cabs of some sort I decided to ask one of the drivers how I could get to Hunt Street in the area of Notting Hill. Much shouting between him and one of the other vehicles ensued until one of them waved to me to approach.

"Will he take me there?" I asked my driver.

"You and as many as he can cram in, Mister! He's the omnibus that goes nearest where you want."

The driver was friendly enough, though I suppose I must have seemed green as he took fourpence from me and told me to climb up onto the knifeboard on the roof. "It's where the men go, Sir – leaves room for the ladies inside. I'll give you a shout when we get near. Not going that close!"

My leg almost let me down as I clambered up the narrow inset steps and swung my valise before me onto the top of the omnibus where a raised piece of wood, which the driver had called the knifeboard, was soon occupied by ten of us. Once the inside was full he cracked his whip in the air and whistled as the huge horse pulled forward and into the busy road. I clung on–almost flying off at points as we swayed and bumped along.

We were at the height of the windows of many tall buildings and looked in on offices, clothing factories, weaving looms, printing presses and families gathered around tables or hearths. Like a theatrical show without sound. The omnibus stopped and started as it picked up and dropped off passengers. Eventually we reached a station called Uxbridge Road where it was stopping and returning back to Kings Cross. A lad leaning against a dark shop front gave me much better directions for a penny than the driver's curt, 'Up there to the left mister!' I turned into a busy enough street called Northland Road then on into a narrow darker lane, repeating to myself, 'Straight up until you pass Gabriel's churchyard then it's on the left'.

Although it seemed a meaner place, people were about and a well-lit inn with what looked like a star as its sign stood out from the shadows, as music rocked it from within and men formed a regular dance in one door and out the second. No one took notice of me as I passed. Then I was there, standing outside a busy corner shop. Light from it cut a path through the dark street behind and a bell rang whenever a customer entered or left. The number above the door was clearly two and I knew I must have found them as my stomach churned. I had come this far and had to go in, whatever may be there.

This was not how I had imagined Etta's place to be. She should be living in one of the tall town houses I had seen from the omnibus, a beautiful garden behind it stretching down to the river, passing her time in a conservatory filled with green plants and tasteful statuary. I straightened my cravat and ran my fingers over my moustache, then entered, hat in hand.

Inside, three people queued before me and I looked around, taking in shelves of myriad commodities piled high with tins and boxes and even some leather work such as belts, harnesses, purses and a pot in the corner containing umbrellas and walking canes. Finally, my eyes lit on the assistant working hard to sell these items and raise a smile in her customers. Etta looked older but steadier in herself somehow. She had a purpose which shone through her transactions and lit up her countenance. Of course, she knew it was me, had seen me when I first entered and with squeals of delight rounded the counter and flung her arms around my neck.

"Thadeus — you came!" she exclaimed stepping back, "Oh, it is so good to see you! Let me close this up and we can go to see everyone else — they are longing to see you too! We only received your letter yesterday. Were you in Prickwillow? Do they hate me?"

"Slow down! Yes of course they do, but me too!"

She took my hand and gave directions to a young lad to finish the last two customers who were behind me, then lock up and take the rest of the evening off. Then she dragged me through to a narrow dark staircase and up to the living quarters above. The parlour we entered reminded me of Ina's family's, not the vicarage one at all. An elderly man in simple clothing sat in a worn armchair near the fire and through the doorway behind him voices floated, one of which made my heart lift.

"He's here, Bridget, Kathleen. He's here!" Etta squealed, pushing past the man as if he was invisible. Then Bridie was there, arms held wide and to my embarrassment I ran straight into them.

"Oh, little Taddy—how's life's adventure taking you?" she muttered into my ear then pulled back laughing. Perhaps home is not a place after all but a person as, for at that moment, I felt I had come home. Bridie's sister Kathleen came in behind her, wiping flowery hands down her apron. The similarity between them was striking but she took pains to point out that she was the older by almost a year.

"Irish twins they call us," she laughed. I wondered why we had never known Bridie had a family. When she went away twice a year we had no idea where she went or who she visited, only thinking of our loss at the time. Kathleen bustled about coming back from the kitchen again with a port for everyone, and Etta continued with the introductions.

"This is Poraic," she pointed out the man in the armchair who grunted,

"Home already young Cathal? Not much work today then?"

Bridie noticing my puzzled look explained, "Poraic is Kathleen's husband but he's away with the fairies, Thadeus—thinks you're his nephew." Everyone laughed except me as it seemed to me that being lost in the whirls of your mind would be a sort of death.

"Can I show Thadeus around, Kathleen? Will you two be fine without my help for a few minutes?"

This seemed to be a joke between the women and Etta dragged me off through a heavily curtained door at the other end of the room.

"You are happy here?" I asked as we entered what seemed to be a surprisingly long corridor.

"I am so happy to be wherever my John is of course and, now I am not so sick, with my work too," she replied.

"You have been ill?"

"Look, Thadeus — really look!" she answered softly and only then did I notice the swell in her stomach.

"Uh-oh —"

"Not — how wonderful — I am to be an uncle?" she teased.

"Of course!" I grasped her hands. "Wonderful Uncle Thadeus!" So, she had not just left for love.

She showed me the room where Kathleen and Bridget slept and, I confess a little strangely, hers and Tom's chamber. Two smaller rooms at the end of the corridor held Poraic and Cathal, who I was to share with. Outside in a small yard you could smell the brick works and iron foundry nearby. This was all overlaid with an animal smell coming from the fields beyond and the regular rattle of engines on the Great Western line. Below all of that there was the constant hum of the city in the distance. Tom worked at a livery stables across the rail bridge a little further down the line and Cathal worked between labouring jobs and helping to run the shop. When we returned to the parlour, Tom was home and Etta ran straight to him. I only remembered him as a boy but he still sported a head of light curls now underlined with a thick orange beard. His smell was all horses and leather as he extended a welcoming hand. Later, as we sat at table sharing a meat pie, the biggest surprise came. The door opened and in walked Will.

The likeness of Cathal to my brother was astounding; a little taller than me with darker hair, no beard or moustache, like Will's large ostentatious one or my neat effort, but sharing both our eyes and face shape. I stood and held out my hand to his but he refused to take it.

"I must needs wash first. Work at the coal yard is a dirty job. Good to meet you though Thadeus."

"Cathal is working there today," commented Poraic conversationally and Bridie confirmed, "Aye he is indeed." This seemed enough to turn his attention back to spearing a potato which had been defying him by slipping around the plate. After the meal the women cleared up and I offered to take a pail down to the yard for water. Etta came with me as

Tom and Cathal disappeared to their rooms. When they returned looking cleaner and somewhat spruced up they asked, "We're away to the Star. Do you want to come?" but I chose to stay with my sister and the woman who had been my mother in truth. There was a question forming in the back of my mind which I did not want to face.

We played a card game called Twenty Five which Bridie and Kathleen won every time having had much practice in it and even Poraic joined in, almost seeming to get his whole mind back for a while. When we had all had enough we drank stout ale and talked of the sisters' arrival in England as young women and of Bridie's meeting with my father at King's Cross station when selling watercress for a few pence a day. His offer of a position of housekeeper and nurse seemed like a gift from heaven to her at the time.

"And I found my gift at the same time, when I met my Poraic!" said Kathleen touching his arm gently. "So, I chose to stay here in London with him. The thought of her working for a married priest was mighty strange to me! He had a wife—so why did he need Bridget?"

Bridie nudged her with some force and quickly changed the talk to Etta's coming baby. I hoped she would have help when the time came and decided I would leave her some money to pay for a proper nurse and midwife. After a few more drinks I began to feel the fatigue that drinking always seemed to lead me to and I had to retire to Cathal's room and fell into a dreamless deep sleep. Waking disorientated in the dark I found him gently snoring beside me, enfolded in most of the blanket. Sleep evaded me for a while after that and I got up to unhook my coat from behind the door and wrap it around me. Thoughts of Ina and Etta became jumbled in my sleep-defying brain. Did Bridie and Kathleen have another sister who was Cathal's mother, and what reason could there be for Cathal and Will's looks? The most obvious answers were strangled by my mind before they could be born.

Next day, Cathal agreed to help Kathleen run the shop and Bridie, Etta and I walked out to visit Kensington and wander in Holland Park. The houses turned to tall, sturdy brick frames, large windows drinking in the winter sun. The pavements were smoothly laid out and clean, brightly dressed women flaunted and chattered, making Etta and Bridie seem quite dowdy in their dresses many times mended and cleaned, mud stained hems and not at all fashionable hats. They, however, seemed not to notice the condescending glances from their fellow sex. We found a small coffee house not far from the park and I insisted on buying whatever they fancied while they watched the passers-by from the window. We talked of how they had left Prickwillow in secret one night and of Etta's exciting trysts with Tom on the riverbank before this. The day became a warm bubble of memory for us all and deep down I could not bring myself to ask the questions which I was beginning to understand the answers to. That evening we ate a stew of rabbit that Tom had caught and cooked. Afterwards, Cathal asked me and Poraic to accompany him to another inn which was a walk away and we left Tom and Etta to keep Bridie and Kathleen company. As we set off I wondered how difficult it would be to keep Poraic from embarrassing us and himself.

The streets were dark but still alive and I found myself smiling at what Ina would think of me walking out to an inn which Cathal had told me was full of Irish, and a good place to sing and enjoy company.

"You are not Irish though?" I enquired, "but your name is, isn't it?"

"You grew up with Bridget, you must have known where she came from?" He fastened Poraic's coat as he spoke. I nodded, not wanting to reveal that Bridie's background was never spoken of in the rectory and we had not asked.

The Bell was a few twisted streets away, some quite dark and others beginning to be reached by the lamp lighter. There were still many people about, openly or skulking in the shadows outside the yellow circles thrown upon the pavements. There were even people whose homes seemed to be outside in the alley ways or the dark corners of stone staircases. The inn stood at the point where the last of those streets cornered onto a wider thoroughfare. Light flooded out from its windows and as the door swung open a blast of warm air laden with tobacco, beer and the noise of what sounded like a hundred voices flooded out. Inside, we pushed our way to a corner table and seated Poraic safely while Cathal and I made our way to the bar.

"I will order—you keep half an eye on him. He can disappear very easily!" Cathal shouted above the din. As we carried three slopping tankards back to his uncle, we found him laughing and talking to someone we could not see, but he took his tankard well enough.

"You are a fine son to look after him so well!"

"Aye, the workhouse or maybe an asylum would do just as well but Kathleen would be lost with him gone."

Over on the other side of the bar a noisy group were

gambling at cards and in the corner a fiddler and accordionist were preparing to play. Any women in the place would have been considered of dubious standing though there were one or two. The singing began with the fiddler picking a tune and Poraic suddenly became clear again, remembering all the words and singing in a fine tenor voice as the men on our neighbouring table joined with him. I felt myself relaxing, letting any worries go and humming along until the musicians took a break. This seemed to switch something in Poraic's head and he began to struggle and shout, "Where's Kathleen gone —where is she? Kathleen, Kathleen........" He pushed Cathal's arm away and turned to me,

"Tell your brother to take me home—we must go. Kathleen wants her boys home!"

To his credit Cathal regained his balance and downing his flagon, caught the old man's hand in his. "I will take him home. Stay there, Thadeus and I will return—it will not take long and the music is good—enjoy it!"

Before I could object they were gone and I was not sure I could remember the way back on my own. A sudden shout arose from the card table and a group of men jumped up, voices loud, fists raised. The publican seemed to have seen it coming and indicated to two burly pot boys to usher the noisy group out. The only way clear was to skirt our table and that is how I found myself eye to eye with Mr. Walsh for the first time since last summer near the beehives in Cornsay Colliery.

Chapter 19

He nodded and gave an amused smile as he recognised me, then pushed his large hat in place and made purposefully for the door behind the rest of the group. As the fiddler struck up again with what sounded like a jig I jumped to my feet shouting, "Stop that man—he's a wanted man!" but my cries were drowned in the suddenly noisy bar. I reached the door only a few seconds later, but the noisy group were already half-way up the street and I could not see if Walsh was still with them. As they passed into a circle of lamplight in the distance I made out what I thought was his large lop-sided hat. He probably felt safe in the knowledge that I could never catch him, but I managed to keep them in my sights, not knowing what I would do if I caught up. No one I passed understood my cries to find an officer and there were none about. Perhaps they knew the group too and did not want to take a chance.   After a few minutes I was beginning to weaken and becoming suspicious that they were leading me on deliberately. They could surely have put on speed and left me far behind. I had to keep up somehow as I knew I had to save Ina from any return of Walsh to the north. I had to face him and warn him to leave her and the Maguires alone.

Then Walsh broke away from the group—I was sure it

was him by his shape and height—and headed down the left fork of the road into a tunnel of dark buildings. Fear of an ambush gripped me but I could not go back— a power without thought was driving me on.

He obviously felt no threat from me and had not bothered to hide in the alley. Somehow we had backtracked and looming out of the dark was the railyard and the high metal bridge which led to the fields and farms beyond. I hung back panting for a few moments and watched his black silhouette mount the open steps and cross to the middle of the bridge. Then he stopped. He was waiting for me. I had nothing I could use as a weapon but I also had no desire for a fight and he could see I was still alone. I mounted the steps with as much purpose as I could muster and faced him. The metal rails of the walk-way were low and I could not hang on to steady myself.

"Well, well! You limped your way after me at quite a pace eh?

"I had to speak with you — no fighting — I just want a promise from you. To leave the Maguires alone."

He laughed then. "Oh dear! But how do you know I will keep my promise? Am I not a wanted man? I need to keep *me* safe lad. There's work to be done here in London."

"Fenian work then."

"Perhaps—or maybe I'll get rich instead. Get one of them big houses near the park—charm a rich lady to spread her legs for me."

His words disgusted me but I had to try again. "Then you are planning to stay here—you should— it's safest here like you say!"

"Then little Ina would be safe too, eh? How was she by the way? How sweet—two little virgins!" He laughed again. "Bit spoilt for me now really!"

I remember rushing for him then—fist raised for a punch when I saw the glint of a blade in his left hand and the punch became a push. He had not been expecting it and his balance went as he flailed, trying to pull me with him—and I faced death as I followed. I have heard that a man's whole life should parade before him at a moment like that but my mind just went blank as I listened to the sickening thud and crunch of him bouncing off a truck in the siding below and landing on the track. Strong hands had righted me by then, pulling me back and my knees gave way as I sank down onto the walkway.

After a moment a voice behind me said, "I saw him jump. He must have known he would not survive." Looking up I blinked for a moment, taking in Will's face.

"It's Cathal —your brother Cathal."

He had returned to the inn as he said he would and had seen me in the distance. Hearing my shouts for an officer he had sent a lad to find one and followed me, catching up as I mounted the bridge. He saw the flash of the knife and ran up behind me just at the moment Walsh fell. Two officers had arrived in the rail yard just before and saw — or perhaps Cathal convinced them that they saw — the man jump to his death. They let me go, praising me for my attempts to save him, asking that I visit the police station the next day, even apologising that I had had to witness the crime of suicide.

When we arrived back at the shop and I had stopped

shivering I noticed for the first time that my hand was bleeding and the knife was nestled in my pocket

I stayed on an extra day, as one benefit of Walsh's death was that the floodgates of information had been opened, and after Bridie and Etta between them had fussed over my hand, we all told our tales.

Leaning back in the train on my return journey to the north, I took out my notebook and wrote as much of it down as I remembered. It was a way of blocking out the memory of my almost fall and sorting out the new images that shaped my early life.

I had to explain Walsh and the Maguire family, mines, plots and Fenians first, then was given a hot brandy and placed in Poraic's armchair by the fire to listen to all their stories.

Bridie had started.

"Your father was young and handsome believe it or not. We were in love for a while and Cathal came along too quickly. Yes—he paid for everything and brought me back to a home here in London where the sisters helped with the birth. They wanted to take my son, but I wrapped him up and escaped through the window at the back of the little chapel. It took a while to find Kathleen and Poraic but as you may have noticed the Irish are many round here and someone knew of them. Charles had said that I could return but only on the strict grounds that I leave my child behind and never speak of him in the vicarage."

Cathal took her hand at that point.

"I had little choice. There was money and a place to live in comfort, and I knew Kathleen would love you, son—as

God did not grant her the gift of children. So, I went back to Prickwillow and took the extra pay for my silence, to send to you, and my two chances a year to spend time with you here. I always knew I would leave forever when the time was right—and my love for Charles had died."

"I knew too," commented Cathal. "She was always full of stories about you, Will and Etta when she came. I am lucky in a way with two mothers and a sister and brother."

"Two mothers who cared!" I muttered under my breath, but Etta had heard and nodded. She told us of her love for Tom as a friend and then more than that, with secret meetings down by the river in the budding spring of the year after I had left.

I looked up at the passing patchwork of fields cut through with busy canals and fast flowing rivers. Perhaps we were all looking for a love returned, even Will with his constant desire for adventure and heroic recognition. The rocking and rattling of the train beneath me began to lull me into a dream until I was there again, hanging over that rail on the dark bridge and Walsh fell up, not down, until his face was right in front of mine and we began to fall back together until my foot kicked out and jerked me awake feeling the scar in my palm throb.

After visiting the police station with Cathal and cementing our story, I had promised to return later in the year and decided I would save some of my salary from the Chronicle to help the family move to a better part of London. I doubted I would go back to Prickwillow. I could not blame Father for his love of Bridie but to condemn another child to grow without a mother as well as Etta, Will and I was too much. It was hard for me to understand where his religion balanced with his conscience and let him go on preaching its values without living them. It was then I remembered Molly. I could write to warn her but she probably did not read and I could not risk Mother reading it to her. Perhaps I would have to return.

Cathal and Tom got together and just before I left they had presented me with a thick piece of leather, perfect to put in my shoe and even out my limp. Everyone celebrated with me as I tried it out in front of the shop. To my amazement it really worked and for the first time since I was seven I could walk without a slight roll. I smiled as I turned my foot around in circles where I sat and remembered the last thing Cathal had shouted to me as the omnibus pulled away.

"Cathal is Irish. My name in English is Charles!"

The journey had seemed to take forever that time but a part of me also felt a bubble of anticipation. I was on my way, back to my job and to Ina. The winter sky closed its grey eyelid on the world as we headed towards the dawn of a new year. Light in the carriage was minimal and outside only distant chimneys here and there lit sparks across the sleeping fields. I shut my book and tucked it into my valise then tried to doze, blocking out Walsh's broken body with the image of Ina on our walk on the fell.

There were no other lodgers in the boarding house and Mrs. Furness expressed surprise at my arrival, laying out a table of ham, pickles and hard cheese for me. The place still held memories of the accursed gun, my illness and my early anxiety but it still felt surprisingly good to mount the stairs with ease and fall into bed and into an unexpectedly deep sleep.   Next morning was the eve of the new year and I indulged in a visit to the barber before arriving at the Chronicle offices. Mr. Creed and I were the only people in the office and we put together a jolly edition of the paper full of puzzles, games and predictions gleaned from Nathaniel's weather man on what to expect, although I could have made them up myself as January is a common time for snow and February more snow and a muddy thaw.

The presses were rolling and after we had put the paper to bed he invited me to an early dinner at his favourite inn. We enjoyed some fine ale and I told him of my recent adventure in London—or as much as I wanted him to know. He revealed that Officer l'Anson had brought him a message, presumably from the undercover police agent, appraising him of Walsh's apparent suicide. There had been an eye kept on Walsh's activities in London.

"But why did they not arrest him when they discovered his whereabouts?" I asked, trying to sound undisturbed and merely curious.

"I think they were on the track of the Fenian group he was involved with down there — hoping they would lead him to whatever they may have been planning. I was surprised that you were involved again I must say."

"My sister lives in an Irish area, that is all. I was not involved in what happened. Merely a drinker in the inn who attempted to do his duty."

"Well, they are happy to believe that, Thadeus, but perhaps you should attempt to stay away from Fenians from now on," he chuckled, in between loading spoonfuls of syllabub into his mouth. "Though we must have some more of those stories from your boy in Cornsay Colliery. Sales numbers have gone up. People are interested—you are settling in well as a reporter, Thadeus. I am happy to have you." I floated back to my lodgings on a cushion of ale, port and those uplifting words.

The next day there was no paper so my next article on the Maguires would be the following week. I would go up to Cornsay on the Sunday, aching to see Ina again after what had felt like such a long absence.

1876

Mrs. Furness and I ate dinner together that day in the big kitchen. Not one for conversation, it was a stony affair and I found myself searching about for anything to say.

"He died you know." Took me by surprise. Did she somehow know Walsh as well?

"Died? Who?"

"Young James. He had the illness you had, but the Lord took him."

"J-James? No—not Jim?"

"Yes and him so young," she said, as if in rebuke to my own thoughtlessness in recovering.   Suddenly the food seemed to lose its attraction and I excused myself and made to leave when she said with a lift, "I've got the room rented mind. That's the main worry fixed."

Upstairs, I sat on the bed for a while in the January gloom and thought about the smallness of life. Will, Thomas and three babies as well as poor Jim—sometimes it seemed like it had only just arrived and was gone in a second. Still in somewhat of a despond, I took the afternoon train up to Durham hoping my reunion with Ina would lift my spirits.

Arriving at the station in Esh I was the only passenger descending from the train and the winter gloom added to the puffing monster of the pit, crouching behind the rows of houses. The figure in a long coat who awaited me however was not Ina, but her father. Thoughts of illness, disaster or banishment from her presence vied with each other in my head as I approached him.

"Good day Mr. Vail. I hoped you would be coming." He nodded, then indicated that we should walk along together. For a while I fell in step with him in silence until I could not resist breaking it,

"I have news for you Mr. Maguire. Good news."

He took a suck on his pipe. "Aye, Kevin Walsh—he's dead. I know."

"But how—?"

"I'm still a Fenian, lad—there's contacts all over. He was a bad un true enough but I wonder what drove him to take his own life?" He stopped puffing tobacco and looked straight at me. So, I told him the whole story—the truth of it. By the time I had finished we'd reached a carriage parked below the beehive run up rails and he suggested we climb inside.

"You know I should trade truth for truth here," he said. "My story of bravery at trying to save my friend's father was not the whole truth either."

"The one I printed in the paper?"

"Just the one! I did not try and save him. I stole his coat and boots—his bag, and what little food he had. I pushed him over in the boat then just watched him go."

I could think of little to say.

"You must try and understand what hunger without end is like. You become a walking empty ache until the desire for food is overtaken by the want to live. At all costs to live. Nothing—no rules, no customs, no boundaries count any longer. You just keep on walking."

The silence when he had finished was broken by a wracking cough which he managed to control with his pipe.

"Then the anger came. We reached England where all would be better, a place like Tir na Nóg— but it wasn't. People took us for foreigners and lazy, drunken ones at that. Oh— there was many a fight I got into—and many a drink I took too!" He laughed then, "but two things saved me— Mary who loved me, and meeting up with people who had lived through the same things, and wanted to save my country from it ever happening again."

"Fenians you mean?" I asked, somewhat incredulous as surely they were violent criminals, not anyone's saviour.

"Aye—not the violence though. We only played at being soldiers really—you cannot believe in the soul of Éire without the show of wanting to fight for it."

I felt then that he was allowing me into the depths of himself, but to take out my notebook and pencil would break the spell. He pulled a small blue stone from his pocket and turned it absently in his fingers. "This is my token of luck you know. Thanks to God and all the powers that be—you saved us from the plot which the likes of McMahon and Walsh wanted. You saved us all from the consequences of it—even if you did not know the full shape of things."

There seemed nothing I could say to that as, just as he had said, I had not known at the time any part of what was happening.

"Well—many happy days to come, eh? I have my family here and will never have to carry them stiff and bone thin down to a crowded graveyard." He got up to move then. "Perhaps a love will change you too one day?" and we climbed down together. That was the only reference to Ina. We walked on back to the street and talked of the weather and vegetables he had sewn for the spring to come.

The family were gathered as usual with the extra presence that time of Thomas and Sean. Ina sat opposite me making my fingers itch to reach out and touch her face. She smiled as friendly as ever, but I wondered had she been told to stay at home. The brothers had to take turns in sharing the last empty chair and I realised I still held them in some awe as I was not sure they had forgiven my intervention in their Fenian plans, even though they could have been languishing in Newcastle gaol without it. Taking out the leather notebook in which I kept Michan's story and a couple of good pencils, I placed the bag at my feet and nodded for him to begin. By the end of Kieran's death scene, a couple of the ladies were openly sobbing and there was a general manly clearing of throats until the youngest Maguire piped up,

"I not dead—are I, Da?" which provoked a round of laughter and broke the sombre mood as Mary scooped him up to reassure him.

It was Thomas who requested a tale this time. "C'mon Da—I've heard there's been a legend from the old country every time young Thadeus was here! Let's have one for the true Fenians now!" He laughed as if joking but I noticed the glance that went between Michan, Sean and their father. He chose not to rise to any provocation however and lit his pipe slowly before beginning.

'About the year 1790 there was a young man who

resided in County Limerick. He was a handsome chap, a writer and a dreamer—a poet too. He was a clever and witty rhymer in the Irish language and had the deep poet eyes that were part of his gift to help him influence female minds.

One day while travelling far from home he came upon a welcoming looking farmhouse and feeling weary, stopped and asked for a drink of milk and a place to rest. The farmer's daughter, a young and pleasant looking girl herself, would not give him admittance as she was all alone. He fixed his earnest gaze on her for some time then turned and walked away to lean for a while on a tree just watching her until finally he turned and left. The girl, who had not stopped watching all this, began to follow him as if in a dream until her father and maids from the house, who had returned from the fields, began to call her back. Turning round she saw them, but the poet quickened his steps and she did the same as if pulled on strings towards him.

As they hurried after her one of the maids saw a piece of paper tied to the tree branch where the poet had been resting and pulled it down to read out of curiosity. Instantly the girl stopped, became quite still and allowed her father to lead her back to the house. She told them that she had felt drawn by an invisible force and would have followed the man through the world for her life seemed to be bound up in his. But suddenly the spell had been broken and then she knew her father's voice and how strangely she had acted."

At this point Michan pulled a piece of paper from his pocket and unfurled it between us on the table.

'The paper written in blood contained these five mysterious words;

Sator

Arepo

Tenet

Opera

Rotas

They can be read from left to right or up and down and, when written in blood with a pen made of an eagle's feather, they form a charm which it is said no woman can ever resist.'

The wondering silence that followed was broken by Mary, "Well 'tis the very note you gave me in my father's yard that time. I might have known it was a spell, Michan Maguire!"

Then suddenly we were all standing, laughing and pushing the chairs and table back before taking our farewells. I tried to position myself beside Ina but her sister Peig got between us.

"Come on! I'll to the station with you two. I need to walk off that evil spell meself now!"

Then we were swiftly out of the front door, Ina and Peig adjusting their shawls and moving to each side of me. My rising excitement slumped. There would be no chance to be alone with Ina and all the past weeks of dreaming of her touch would have to suffice. Just before we reached the station she took my arm and deftly pushed something in my pocket, bidding me a chaste farewell. I did not look at it until safely on the train. She had written neatly on a piece of a brown paper bag such as contain purchases from a grocery shop like Etta's,

Come early next week. Get off at Esh Winning. We can walk back.

With a glimmer of hope I placed it back carefully, meaning to read it as often as I could before then. The rest of the way I pondered Michan's story. Presumably I was meant to be the young poet and Ina the subject of his fairy spell, rescued by her father. He was always excellent at picking just the right tale to keep me on edge.

Chapter 20

In the office the next day we were treated to the return of Nathaniel Parkes, back from his term of agricultural news gathering and not changed at all. Henry had grown his hair into a poetic flop which caused him to flip his head at constant intervals while he tried out a melancholy demeanour to go with it. This evaporated quickly when I introduced him to the love spell from Michan's latest tale.

"This would work! By Jove! I will try this today. Oh, Thadeus, it could be the answer to my sad love problems!"

I refrained from pointing out that it did not seem to be working so well for mine. It felt warm and familiar to be part of the morning meeting again and I was pleased to note that Mr. Creed adopted a distant attitude to Nathaniel—sending him on a job to interview a local gardener about the problems with frost he was encountering—and ignoring the way he left the room without comment, loudly shutting the heavy door behind him. Henry was off to speak with a local shop owner who had grave doubts about the freshness of the water in the well near his establishment, particularly as it was drawn from under the ground near the Quaker cemetery and had a strange taste.

The two most interesting tasks I was given that week

were to visit a local poet and artist, and to interview the workers in a distillery about a persistent ghost. The artistic poet actually worked in the stuffy confines of the large bank on the High Street but had just had a book of his drawings published and Mr. Creed deemed them worthy of a piece in the Chronicle. I had to walk out of town a little way to reach his dwelling and was surprised to find that, like him, it confounded expectations. He was younger than I had expected and with a cheerful manner not always common to those who work in a bank. The house itself stood at the corner of a row of comfortable looking, well-appointed buildings but unlike them, it ended the row of Prospect Place with a perfectly rounded shape. I was intrigued to find how its dimensions could accommodate any furniture and hoped I would discover the answer. A cheerful looking maid answered the door and ushered me in. After introductions he took me into a disappointingly regular shaped parlour and sent for tea.

His pictures were fine drawings of local and country scenes and his enthusiasm for the area and his travels within it shone through, coloured by an endearing sense of humour. We talked for too long in front of the roaring crackle of the open hearth before he had to leave for the bank and I realised I must hurry to get back to the office in time for our illustrator to copy out a couple of the pictures to get in print that evening. On the way back, I realised I had forgotten to ask him about rounded furniture and circular rooms.

Later in the week, a very different assignment had found me in Forster's Yard, a dank place where mainly wine and spirit merchants traded. I was to talk to an employee about another sort of spirit which many of the workers claimed to have encountered and even spoken with. Mr. Frederick Burn, slight and short, dressed in workman's garb and what could have been considered an overly large apron, came out from behind a counter where his bald head had been shining just above its edge and motioned me to follow him back into the warehouse space behind the shop front. The damp darkness within held an overwhelming smell of alcohol and was home to hidden angles from where a spectre could have jumped out on us at any moment. We stopped at one of these and Mr. Burns began his story.

"I have seen him—just here—four times now. I believe he is a soldier by his dress but it is an ancient sort of uniform. He sometimes speaks."

"Can you recall his words?"

"Not exactly. He seems to be agitated as if he is running from someone and looks over his shoulder to see if they are following then calls something like, 'Not me' and other garbled sounds before he vanishes."

"Vanishes!"

"Yes Sir, 'tis the nature of ghosts so I believe."

"But were you not shocked by all of this?"

"I was the first time. I had to run to the Green Tree Inn for comfort and company, but after that I got used to old Johnny—which is what we call him."

Three other employees had joined us by then and they all seemed entirely sincere in supporting Mr. Burns' evidence with their own tales. I decided this may need further investigation so asked if I could return later and pass some time alone to see if I could also witness the phenomenon. So it was that I found myself at six that evening waiting patiently for a figure in red coat, long boots and a tricorn hat to step out of the wall. I waited for over an hour and began to notice that the more I stared at the wall the more I seemed to catch movement in the corner of my vision, although no soldier stepped out and passed me by. Eventually it had become too cold to wait and I left, a little disappointed with the publicity shy shade. I knew I had enough to write as disturbing a tale as one of Mr. Dickens' however, and left for the nearest inn and a warming flip of hot ale, brandy and sugar.

Before I knew it, I was arriving back in Esh Winning on Sunday afternoon. Foregoing another meal with Mrs. Furness, I had eaten at the Red Lion again and taken the early afternoon train. I held Ina's note safely in my great coat pocket and repeated the spell in my head in keeping with the rattle of the wheels, concentrating on it so much I almost missed the stop. Passing the bench where the signal was supposed to have been left, what felt like a lifetime ago, I saw her leaning against a wall, engrossed in a copy of the Northern Chronicle.

"Reading the latest by that amazing writer Thadeus Vail by any chance, Madam?"

"Oh, but it is him in person! I am so privileged!" She smiled and reached up to kiss me.   Relief ran through me then as I had thought she may have been warned off me in some way or merely lost the attraction we had originally felt for each other, like my parents. She pulled away and wrapped her shawl tighter around her hair.

"Come—say nothing. I have a surprise."

Linking arms, we set off down a street which could have been in any of the pit villages by the shapes and sizes of its houses, and turned down a lane which snaked round a bend in the distance. To my surprise, we stopped by one of the wooden yard gates and she pulled us both inside, then taking out a large key she opened the back door to the house.

"Come on!" she reassured my anxious look, "It is my aunt and uncle's house—where Martha lives. They have taken her to visit Ailis and her babe today. We have at least an hour alone. We are alone!" I found I had no words to argue.

Desire rose from my lower stomach and sent sparks up and down through all my parts. The curtains were pulled across the front window and the roll out bed, left ready for the family's return, invited us. For the first time, we could re-move all our clothing and discover every part of each other's trembling bodies. Ina showed me what gave a woman pleasure and ran her hands all over my nakedness until I could wait no longer and we fell together onto the bed. Afterwards, a per-fect languor was spreading through me when she realised that it had become dark outside and loud voices were approaching down the street. She dressed herself in a second and before I had a time to speak, threw my drawers at me, hissing,

"Quickly—we have lost time—perhaps you need a ser-vant to dress you? Hurry!"

Once in the lane I tied my second shoe and tucked in my cravat. Ina seemed to have managed much more quickly than me and I vaguely wondered whether she had much prac-tise in dressing at speed. The walk to Cornsay Colliery seemed longer than I remembered it and a happy heaviness slowed me down. "Why don't we run away together?" I remember ask-ing— but she just laughed.

"Very well—catch me, Thadeus!" and set off running there and then. When I caught her the kiss, as forfeit, slowed us down again. At last we reached the top of her street and she went ahead as I waited, having agreed that we would make it seem that she had missed me at the station. The family believed that she had been to Esh Winning to measure for a dress that her mother was making for someone there and had been held back for tea with the woman and so missed the later train that I should have been on and just went straight home. Everyone was assembled as usual when I knocked at the door and I made a show of disappointment at not finding Ina at the station.

When we had all settled, I hoped my hair and moustache were not showing signs of my earlier activity as there was no obvious mirror at the Maguires to check this in. Michan began the next step of his tale after I had readied my notebook and pencil. It was of journeying north and the many problems he had faced before settling with Mary and beginning his own family. The way they had to hire a cart and throw everything in it when his bond at a mine was up and move to new masters, new dwellings, new friends and sometimes enemies to their Irish ways.

For some reason I felt both hungry and tired and had to stifle a yawn at times, hoping he, Thomas and Sean did not take my lethargy as boredom. I thought perhaps we would not get a tale from the fairy powers that time but Ina spoke up—perhaps to cause a distraction,

"Do you have a tale from the Thuatha for us, Da? A shorter one maybe so the children can get their sleep?" She did not look at me but I knew what she meant. Michan took a few moments to refill his pipe then began.

"Hundreds of years ago there was a famous tune called

Moraleana that was played on the hills by the fairy pipes. A human piper passing that way learned it from them and played it with beauty, but was told he could play it only three times in his life but never a fourth or a doom would fall on him. He played it for a great audience and all the people applauded the wonderful fairy melody. Then one day he joined a contest with another piper—a contest of supremacy— and to make sure he won, he played Moraleana again and all watching were entranced by its beauty once more. So pleased was he to win that he played it one more time for the assembled people forgetting the fairy warning, and he suddenly turned deathly pale, the pipes dropped from his hand and he fell lifeless to the ground. For nothing escapes the fairies; they know all things, and their vengeance is swift and sure."

Thomas nodded sagely, "Aye nothing escapes the fairies eh, Da?" and Kevin sighed and stretched,

"Well, tis us away to our beds—let's hope they do not find us in our dreams!"

He scooped up Eliza and Ailis wrapped her shawl more tightly round the sleeping baby.

"Goodnight to you all. This new one's making me sleep without any fairy help and with two already to look after I need as much sleep as I can get!"

As they left, everyone else began the ritual of moving the chairs and pushing the table back ready for the drop down bed. Michan turned to me as if he had just remembered something.

"Next time, I will find you a beautiful tale and tell of all the good that came into my life. It will cheer us all. Be happy now, lad—do not wait for good to come to you—remember nothing escapes the fairies!"

I left alone as Ina had been held back by Mary to discuss the sewing task she had been measuring for and I hoped her story telling was as good as her father's. Though I walked slowly, she never came out to catch me.

A few days later I bumped into Nathaniel entering the office, swaggering with a newly affected cane.

"Well, your fun is over, eh?"

"Is it?" I asked, looking up from where Caligula had been rubbing his ears around my hand.

"A friend from Barnard Castle went to work on the Durham Chronicle. He advised me to buy it and keep up with other news in the area." He held it out to me and waited for my reaction as he pointed to a small paragraph in amongst a page of advertisements, people selling livestock and even canary chicks.

Fatal Accident at Cornsay Colliery. On Wednesday morning, a man named Michan Maguire met with his death at the above colliery. At half past eight o'clock a large quantity of blue stone fell upon him injuring him in such a fearful manner that death took place before he could be extricated.

Both Maud and Nathaniel stared at me after I had thrown the paper to the ground and tottered back against Queen Victoria repeating, 'blue stone, blue stone, blue stone' until I managed to straighten up and groan, "Nothing escapes the fairies—of course it doesn't!"

Part 3

1876–1890

Chapter 1 - Ina Maguirre

It was late morning and the wash was on when Joe Martyn came gasping to the door, himself as black as the coal he hewed, with only two white circles for his eyes. I had been bashing the sheets in the dolly tub and dreaming of Thadeus' touch, looking forward to the following Sunday and finding ways to be with him alone before he joined us all to write Da's story. In the newspaper he was just named as 'An Irish Miner', which is what he had wanted to be, but the stories were written well. Thadeus was indeed a good writer—that I will always grant him, for all that some of my family had thought him high and mighty.

Loud thumps had shaken the front door as Joe called, 'Mary, Mary, come quickly!' For a second Ma and I had looked at each other then, with hands dripping, we ran. You understand a miner does not come off shift before his time, so we almost knew what his news would be. In fact, it was the worst—no injury, broken back or legs, no gas or burning—Da was dead. We left Kieran with Mrs. Carrigan next door and ran with Joe up to the adit entrance where Ben Martyn and

Enda Kennedy were standing, dazed, with a stretcher hung between them.

Blood was everywhere, pooling on the ground, turning the tarpaulin black and painting the men's fists crimson. Worst of all Da's hand and arm hung down, seeming to move with their footsteps. Before I could stop her Mammy ran forwards and took hold of it, pressing it to her cheek and sobbing, 'Michan—wake up love—wake up—wake up —'. No one stopped her but it was that gesture which started sobs racking like sickness through my body until I fell to the ground and wrapped my arms around her skirt begging, 'Stop, stop, stop it!'

She had to leave go when the overseer turned up and told her that they must take him away and place him where the doctor could be called to him, and Joe and I dragged her off screaming, 'Doctor, doctor? He is not dead then? You can save him!'

The doctor did arrive an hour later, during which time they had placed a guard on the shed door. The strength she had grew with each sob, and a sort of madness overcame her as she cried out that he would be cold, he should not wake in the dark, we could not hear him locked in there and then just the word, 'Alone, alone—' over and over. When he had examined him, the doctor came out and told us quite directly, "Your husband is dead Madam. The stone of the roof had fallen on his head and crushed it. He died instantaneously. Good day to you all." And placing his top hat back in position, he sauntered off to the owners' office with his report. A small crowd of women had gathered by then and surrounding Ma and I in sympathy, walked us back to the house which would never be his again.

That evening, we all sat at the table while Thomas spoke and Ailis sat with her arm around Mammy. A wild thought that Thadeus would be here soon and Da could start his story spun around my head until I almost said, 'Tell him to give us one of his happy tales this time!', then remembered he would never be there again. Thomas claimed his place as head of the family and laid out the plan of how it would go for the rest of the week. He was always good at being practical and had already talked to Father Lodge and the undertaker. First thing, we women would go up and wash the body then he would be taken to the undertakers on a cart and returned to us on Sunday evening to lay out, until we all walked to Esh New Winning behind him the next day.

"He loved to walk," I said.

"Aye, so do we all, until a mine falls in on us," Sean followed in a bitter voice.

"Leave him!" called Ailis as Peig made to slap him for speaking out in front of Ma.

"We should all go to our beds now — hard as it is. You men are on the early shift tomorrow and we have a dark task of our own to carry out. Will you sleep with Ma and Kieran the night, Ina?"

I nodded, not relishing it. But I was exhausted and it was always warmer sleeping in the kitchen, even if Da might come back and find me in his place. As I drifted off eventually I remembered that I had not thought of Thadeus since the tragedy unfolded. Mammy slept surprisingly well, though woke, like both of us, to the feeling that the news of Da's death had just broken anew. Mrs. Carrigan took Kieran again and we set off to the shed after breakfast. I had found myself very hungry and it was a relief before we left to play with Kieran and spoon his porridge in with one hand while eating mine.

The shed was dark enough to need candles to see and once they were lit we could never unsee. From the shoulders down, Da looked as he had always done but above that was a red pulp in place of a head which had hardened and stuck crust-like to his shirt collar and jacket. Ma knelt and kissed the place where his mouth should have been and then we began. Carefully we removed his clothes and began to wash the stiff coldness of his limbs. I had never seen him completely naked and he looked so thin. I tried not to compare him with the warm muscles of Thadeus' body such a short time before that day. The hope that no one could read my thoughts suddenly seemed amusing and caused me to giggle. To my surprise this spread, affecting all but Ma, and we agreed that Da would be amused, not shocked. After all, he had bathed after his shift in the tin bath almost every day and even if Ma had shooed us out during the process, he had often wandered about wrapped in a towel while she fetched his clean clothes.

It took a lot of rags to remove the bloodied coal dust but finally we were ready to dress him again. The task was difficult because of his head but we worked together and finished by wrapping Ma's shawl around what was left of it and, leaving her to say a final goodbye. The rest of us women left. Outside it was a sharply sunny day and I breathed deeply, raising my face to catch its weak winter rays. I kept my hand closed over the blue stone that had fallen out of his pocket when we turned him. I knew what it meant to him as he had told me on many walks out to the fell and even convinced me for a while that it could do magic as well as the fairies in his tales. I made a wish on it that he would go back to Eire now and find them all there waiting for him, Ailis, Ilene and his brothers. We used the pump at the end of the street to clean ourselves up, then left for home.

The next two days seemed to twist time like a chewed tobacco plug and spit it out as a mush. The worst jobs were done already and I was delegated to sit by the door and answer all the callers who came to give their wishes to Ma. The space between these was hard to fill. I tried imagining that the next person would be Thadeus and we could at least entertain each other with talk, or perhaps it would be Mr. Ferenc, one of the mine owners, with a huge bag of money, or even the Queen with humble thanks for her roaring palace fires, but my mind kept drifting to the last time Da and I had been alone. It was an evening after Christmas and Ma had gone to visit her brother and his family in Esh Winning. I had put Kieran to bed and we were left alone by the fire for an hour before he went out to the inn.

"Tell me about being in love, Ina," he said leaning back and stretching his socks towards the grate.

I should not have been surprised, for Da had always been able to see how things went with me and it was obvious he guessed something was happening with Thadeus.

"Do you not remember, Da?" I laughed— trying to think of a way to change the subject.

"Aye! All too well, lass! That's why I'm asking."

"I am not sure. I will tell you when I know."

"I'll put it another way—what is happening between you and Mr. Vail? Is there anything I should know?"

I was convinced it was confusion about my feelings that coloured my face but Da knew it was more than that.

"Can you see yourself running off to be a fine wife in a big house, or do you want this life with a hardworking miner and many children to raise, lass—which is it?"

Then I knew suddenly. "None of those, Da. First I want to travel away from here, learn more things than just reading and sums. Do other tasks than washing and sewing. See the sky in other lights."

He was silent for a moment then leaned forward, tapping the plug from his pipe bowl and said, "Well, those are wonderful things and I think you could do all of them, Ina—but take care not to tie yourself up in chains before the chance comes." Then he pulled his boots on and went off to meet his friends in the Oddfellows. Looking back, perhaps I should have listened.

Eventually, those dark sad days had rolled by and the place was almost ready to receive the body for the vigil night.

The letter arrived that Saturday evening. By that time, I had cried most of the tears inside me and could talk of him more calmly. It was creased and stained from its long journey and Jimmy McEwan the postman was reluctant to pass it over from the grasp of his tobacco stained fingers, seeing it was addressed to Da and feeling the buzz of the words trapped inside. It bore only his name and the words, Cornsay Colliery, England.

"It's from America—all the way across the sea and—"

"Thank you, Jimmy—I'll take it now!" I snapped, almost

ripping the amazing news in bits before it had a chance to escape whole from the envelope.

Ma was inside finishing the job of getting the parlour ready for the coffin—scrubbing and cleaning everything that wouldn't fall apart or crumble under the strength of her arm. Carrying on was what she'd always done. Keeping wherever we had moved to next as clean as she could, up and down in the night for so many babies, then later for the end of different shifts with a meal, whatever time it was. She had loved him once, in the way of dreams and moonlight and summer sunsets; the fact of Kieran's birth confirmed that. But it was mainly work that shaped their lives by then — and work became her comfort in those empty days.

Kieran slept safely in his crib so I shoved the crumpled letter in my apron pocket and told her I would go round the back and check the washing hanging in the lane. It was early dark and the weather was cold and damp like a fret from the sea. I had needed my shawl. Hidden by flapping bedclothes and underwear I could open the letter and read it in peace.

Katherine her name was—Katherine Winter it had been—although it was now Maguire. The paper inside the envelope was fine and the writing close and neat. It was written to Da, but I would have had to help him read it. I often wonder if it would have changed his life as it did mine.

Dear Michan, it began— though he was a stranger to her really —

I am your nephew James' wife. We live in America, in a place called Massachusetts not far from a city called Boston and own a farm and several properties here. James' father is Patrick Maguire and his uncle is Tom Maguire. The family are well respected here and your father Thomas feels it is time to send for you. He does well for his great years and enjoys having his family around him. He lives with James and I now and another reason to write is that we all look forward to the child I am bearing in the fall.

The war is long behind us and those difficult times are gone. Tom, my brother in law, fought in the Fighting Ninth Irish platoon and was injured but manages well now— even without sticks. Times were hard for your father when he first arrived and made a perilous journey down from New York, finding labouring work in Boston. Please believe he went back to find you all in Ireland after he was freed from prison for joining a group accused of stealing bread, but could find no one to tell him whether you had left or perished. He could not read or write and has found the learning of those skills a hard task. He still tells stories of a ship full of fever and death and we are all so grateful that he survived and found his older sons in New York.

Recently he has talked a lot of his first family and it was a great surprise to meet a man this last harvest time travelling for work who told us about you, Michan. He had been a labourer at a mine in the north of England the previous year where he became acquainted with another Thomas Maguire. Through him he heard stories of Ireland passed down by his own father and it became clear that you and he must be one and the same person. That you live is a wonder to Grand- Father-in-Law, and he hopes you can also put us in contact with any other members of his family that live as well.

This letter contains tickets for your passage. If you have need of any more please reply by return of post and we should receive your letter within a fortnight, God speed.

As I write here on the porch, birds sing and a warm breeze ruffles the corn in the far field. Tom's grandsons ride their ponies around the paddock nearby and little Jimmy waves to me, pointing to the thicket where he says the fairies live! I understand you have a life there, but please consider your father's kind offer—there is space and work for you here and life is good.

She finished with; *your affectionate niece, Katherine.*

Underneath, a shaky hand had penned the name, *Thomas.*

I held her words to my racing heart, trying to contain it in my chest. I made two choices then—to keep this from Ma until after the funeral— and to be there on that porch with Katherine as soon as I could.

Chapter 2

By the time we had walked behind his coffin all the way to Esh New Winning and into the church the next day, filling the front benches, we were all exhausted. Father Lodge had stayed a while to pray with us and then we all sat around the wooden box that was Da, with Thomas at the head and told tales of his life to each other. We could not have an open coffin and I heard Sean and Da's marrow, Ben, whisper quietly together about 'the head' and 'great distress'. The church had filled up quickly and we turned to watch the box being carried slowly by his sons and sons in law and two grown nephews from Ma's family. Da and I knew that this could always be his end but a trace of hope lived side by side with this reality. Each shift, a miner kept his hope alight with his lamp or candle until the next bath by the fire and an hour or so with his family.

A split in the cloud outside caused a shaft of light from the window to bathe us as we sat down, and my mind floated up, away from the sobs of my sisters and Ma to drift in those walks of childhood. He had loved to walk out into the countryside as if there was a journey he could never quite finish. Sometimes all three of us girls would hike out with him onto the fells away from the soot and smells of mines, tall chimneys and the mechanical sounds of industry. Sometimes the boys would be with us too, but whatever happened I always managed to keep him company. I loved the crispness of the air, the calls of lapwing, curlew and golden plover, the wind ruffling my madly springing hair and the lift on his shoulders when my legs got too tired to return to wherever home was. Some winter nights when he wasn't on shift, we would cram together at the hearth and listen to his stories of the Sidhe, Fion Machual and fairy boats carrying dead heroes and stolen princesses. It had been a touch of magic to repeat those times with Thadeus later on. I remembered trying to teach Da to read and how he longed for a fairy wish to make it easier. Then he would slip into tales of his brothers and little sister Ilene, though when I asked him where they had gone to when grown he would only say they were in the fairy halls, dancing and feasting. This would sometimes raise the anger in him and he would leave the house to meet Enda Brennan and their friends at the inn.

Before I had even noticed, the Mass had come to an end and we were following the coffin out to the hole. The miners' relief fund and the owners, to cover their own guilt, had provided enough money for the funeral and there would even be a gravestone. I could not say goodbye to him again after the wake of the previous night and the last hour in the shed so as soon as Ma had thrown the handful of earth clattering down onto the lid, I left them and wandered up to the front of the building. Musing over the best time to break the news about America to her and the family as I went, I did not notice Thadeus until I bumped into him.

Although I had wanted so much to wrap my arms

around him, I had to push him away—there were too many witnesses at that moment. I suppose I had forgotten that I would have to tell him too and though part of me ached to beg him to accompany me, I knew deep down that he would not want to leave the new life he was making for himself. He wore a smart great coat and a new hat, his hair tamed with that oil he used and moustache shaped neatly; he carried the satchel that came to all our Sunday evening sessions and held the leather notebook in his hand. For a moment I could think of nothing to say.

"Oh, Ina!" he said softly and then I cried. He fumbled out a large white kerchief from his pocket and handed it to me as I struggled to control the tears I had not thought were left.

"I hope this is clean!" I sobbed.

"Well, it isn't now I think!"

We both smiled after that and he asked me to walk a little way with him.

"I want to give you this." He held out the notebook to me, "It is all of his story and his tales. You should have it. Perhaps one day you can read it again and remember him."

"What will you do now? With no reason to visit—until the next tragedy of course."

"I could have a reason—if you want me to."

So, I knew that was when I must tell him. "Da got a letter. On Saturday. I opened it."

"That must be sad for you all—to receive a letter for someone who is gone," he said in sympathy.

"No, Thadeus—it was surprising but not sad. His father,

who he looked for but could never find, is in America. Alive! He is alive!"

"Well, that is—"

I took his hand to stop him saying anything else. "He has sent tickets. Ma does not know yet—but I am going. To live in America!"

"You have decided so soon? Are you sure it is not just the shock and grief that have affected your thinking? To leave everything behind!"

"No, no! You can come too. There are enough tickets. Imagine how your life could be—all the newspapers you could work for!" I could see then what I had known already through the disappointment in his eyes, the slumping of his shoulders.

"But Ina, my life is just beginning here! I have my sister and her family to keep an eye on too. I could not leave it all now."

The rest of the funeral party were beginning to catch up then so we dropped our hands and walked in silence for a while. I had not known just how hard it would be to end our dream of love. To let Thadeus go.

"Remember all that time ago when I told you to beware of fairy kisses?"

"I should have believed you but you had already enchanted me!"

"You cannot follow me though—can you, Thadeus? The magic was not that strong, was it?"

"You could stay here and marry me. Be my wife, Ina!"

For a moment I was thrown, but I was young and the future I wanted then was not as anyone's wife— even his.

"I have to take this chance to travel—to fly this place.

I cannot marry you but you always have my love to keep in your memory." My reply confused me as well as Thadeus and he looked away, clearing his throat to disguise tears.

"Look, Ina! There is our tree—the one where you told the story of Cliodhna the Banshee and her magic birds, when we lay underneath it. So now I'm drowning too, like her."

"Oh Thadeus—"

We had spoken in hushed voices but Peig had caught us up.

"Da would be pleased that you came to his funeral, Thadeus—even if it was just to write a story on it for the Chronicle," Peig was accomplished at the double pointed remark and even though she was married, I had always suspected that she was jealous of our relationship however secret we had tried to keep it. She dropped back with a flounce and took Ma's other arm—the one Ailis was not holding.

After the storm of the following week, when I read Katherine's letter first to Ma and then to the whole family called together by Thomas, life had become an exciting bubble, only popped occasionally when I lay alone at night and thought of Thadeus. He had left for the train when we reached Cornsay Colliery again, his face a study of sadness, his steps surprisingly even but with no spring in them. I felt something break inside me as he swung up onto the train and did not look back. His piece in the Chronicle on Da's funeral I still keep with me all these years later, but I did see him one more time before I left for Liverpool. Thomas, as head of the family, had forbidden my adventure, but eventually Sean had chosen to come too and this had finally led to his permission.

"America is not Esh you know, Ina. You cannot go and

come back easily. You must say your farewells forever," he explained, as if I was a small child.

"I will not do that, Thomas! If a person can travel there, then they must be able to come back. I will see you all again and perhaps you can come and find me there too?"

He shrugged and sighed as if there would be no explaining to someone as young as me and it set my plans even firmer than they had been before. Looking back, perhaps he and Thadeus had both been right. The thrill of planning such a huge adventure did carry me through the sadness of those dull days after Da's funeral— and I have not seen any of them again since.

The following Friday, I decided to visit Darlington in the hope of one final, calmer farewell with Thadeus. I told Ma I was up to Durham to take measurements for the last time from a woman who was after a new dress for her second wedding. I fully intended to do this then hop on the train south, but in the end I had to rush it on the way home later. My final task for Ma.

February still held its frozen grip of the landscape when I descended the train steps onto the platform in Darlington. Steam clouds wrapped around me turning into grey layers of fog as I left the station. This thinned as I reached the old bridge that spanned the frozen river and walked up the hill into town. The market was already busy but I hurried past, heading for the Chronicle's ornate doors, the warmth inside a contrast to the ice hard day. As I shook out the crystals from my shawl I was surprised by the excited shout of, 'Ina! It is so good to see you again!' and was engulfed in a warm embrace.

Maud stood back to appraise me further while keeping a hold on my cold hands.

"My, but you are thinner I believe and so pale! The death of your Father must weigh heavy with you all."

"He would want us to remain of strong purpose, Maud — the struggle of life must go on." I sighed. It was still hard when anyone mentioned Da's death at that time not to be thrown into a vivid flash of a mangled face above a coal streaked body and the iron smell of blood congealing on a shed floor.

"Here—come behind the desk with me and I will make you a warm drink and you can rest awhile."

My regret for accepting has eased with time and perhaps it had been for the best that I did not get to leave my gift with Thadeus Vail. People came and went as we talked of brighter things and the hope that my journey would bring a better life, until we were interrupted by a handsome young man peering over the top of the desk with a cheery,

"Why Maud, who is this young lady?"

"Good morning, Henry" she remarked in what sounded like a rebuke of some sort, "This is Ina Maguire, daughter of the poor dead miner and friend of Thadeus. Is he in or returning soon?"

"Oops! You just missed him—gone out on a follow up to a tragic case from last year. If you hurry you may catch him as he will probably be in the market."

Placing his hat firmly on his floppy mane, he made a slight bow to us both and left. Of course, I rushed out straight after him and for a moment could not see Thadeus anywhere but then he came into view facing away from me and holding an animated conversation with a woman who seemed to be selling fruit. I still remember the shape of his shoulders, the way his hair curled on the back of his collar and the sound of his laugh forming a want deep inside me that I had to resist. I knew then that I could never leave him again, the first time still twisted like a pain in my guts and I forced my footsteps away, each one seeming to take forever as the tears blurred my vision.

In the end it took us only ten days to reach Boston and both Sean and I had been excellent sailors. We travelled on the story that I was widowed tragically young but the child had not begun to show by then anyway so it had really not been necessary. It did help though when we reached Greenhills and met our grandfather for the first time. He had been waiting at the gate of the track with his two great grandsons and even in the distance it seemed like Da had come back, white haired and smiling. Katherine's child had been born in the first fall of leaves and Mary four months later, so they grew like brother and sister. We had ten years full of sunshine with four more cousins added over time until the farm became like a school, with me as the teacher. Sean had stayed in Boston and joined a building company which he now owns with his partner.

Once Mary and Michael were old enough, walking them down to the school in town had led to my meeting with Jack.

From the first moments, the constant wonder of a clear sky and clean fresh breezes carried me along and began to heal the worst of my memories. I wrote to Ma and the family often and once or twice they wrote back. She did not want to hear about Grandfather as she still believed he could have returned to his family and taken them with him when he left Ireland in that terrible winter. But she was interested in Katherine and all her babies. Most recently my heart sank when Ailis wrote that Kieran was now a miner. I thought of his little face at the station when Sean and I were saying farewell. I had taken him for a last cuddle from Ma, dipping my face in his flame coloured curls and drinking in his baby smell to store in my memory. To my surprise he had smiled and said, "The fairy stone—no lose it. Da needs it safe."

Now he carries a bait box and pick down into the dark like all the others.

After that ten years, my own resolve had weakened and Jack and I were married at last and moved with our daughter and twin sons here to Boston. Grandfather had died the previous summer and I grieved for the evenings spent sharing tales and songs from the old country with him, but he had a good old age with so much company and twice as many years as his son, Michan.

I am ready now to take up the position of schoolmistress at Jack's school and in the summer vacation we intend to travel and spend some time under different skies. In the evening, we have a porch to sit on and sometimes Mary sits with us while I tell one of Da's tales, or just watch the stars above the city. Often I catch myself watching her too and see them all there, my sisters, brothers, Ma and Da, and just lately—Thadeus Vail.

APPENDIX

A few years ago I started to research my ancestors, and the idea for 'The Blue Stone' began to take shape in my mind.

I discovered that one of my third great-grandfathers,—Michael McCormick,—had died in the mine at Cornsay Colliery when the roof collapsed on his head. The only other facts I had for him were that he was born in county Sligo in the west of Ireland and that by 1851 he was twenty, married to a girl who had come from the same area, and living and working as a miner in the Durham coalfields. Although both my parents were of Irish descent this had never been mentioned by them and they had no knowledge of his name or origins.

My early research into the Famine began to clarify the way Michan's— or Michael's— journey and early life *could* have been, and all the dark times he encounters are taken from first hand reports of the Famine. I cannot know whether he had any actual connection to the Fenians, but it seems a possibility.

The short paragraph from The Durham Chronicle which records his death in the mine in the book, is the actual one. I only managed to get hold of it towards the end of the book and was surprised to find that it says he was killed by 'a fall of blue stone.'

Thadeus Vail is entirely fictional, but my knowledge of the history of Darlington—my home town—in 1875 is incorporated into his story. He illustrates the way the Irish were perceived in England as immigrants, although Ireland at the time was governed by, and part of the UK. I wanted to show that, even when they are forgotten, our ancestors' life experiences roll down through the generations, and have a place in our genetic makeup.

In the words of L Hogan: *'Watch and listen. You are the result of a thousand loves.'*

I am indebted to my tutors and fellow students from Middlesex University M.A. course in Novel Writing. To my family, and to Jane Elgee— who later became Lady Wilde— for her wonderful collection of 'Celtic Magick and Folklore.'

Many thanks for travelling with Michan, Thadeus and Ina!